ed
ds,
el.

ur
s
l,
f
a passion for travel.

**Rely on Thomas Cook as your
travelling companion on your next trip
and benefit from our unique heritage.**

Thomas Cook **pocket** guides

GIBRALTAR

Written and updated by Katherine Rushton

Published by Thomas Cook Publishing
A division of Thomas Cook Tour Operations Limited
Company registration no. 3772199 England
The Thomas Cook Business Park, Unit 9, Coningsby Road,
Peterborough PE3 8SB, United Kingdom
Email: books@thomascook.com, Tel: +44 (0) 1733 416477
www.thomascookpublishing.com

Produced by Cambridge Publishing Management Limited
Burr Elm Court, Main Street, Caldecote CB23 7NU
www.cambridgepm.co.uk

ISBN: 978-1-84848-398-9

First edition © 2008 Thomas Cook Publishing
This second edition © 2011
Text © Thomas Cook Publishing
Maps © Thomas Cook Publishing/PCGraphics (UK) Limited

Series Editor: Karen Beaulah
Production/DTP: Steven Collins

Printed and bound in Spain by GraphyCems

Cover photography © DAVID J SLATER/Alamy

CONTENTS

WHAT'S IN YOUR GUIDEBOOK?

Independent authors Impartial, up-to-date information from our travel experts who meticulously source local knowledge.

Experience Thomas Cook's 165 years in the travel industry and guidebook publishing enriches every word with expertise you can trust.

Travel know-how Thomas Cook has thousands of staff working around the globe, all living and breathing travel.

Editors Travel-publishing professionals, pulling everything together to craft a perfect blend of words, pictures, maps and design.

You, the traveller We deliver a practical, no-nonsense approach to information, geared to how you really use it.

THE AUTHOR

Katherine Rushton lives in London with her Gibraltarian husband. She works as a full-time journalist for a trade magazine, and contributes to *Time Out*, the *Telegraph*, the *Guardian* and BBC News. She used to be resident on the Rock, where she worked for the local newspaper, the *Gibraltar Chronicle*.

● *A stunning view from the Rock of Gibraltar*

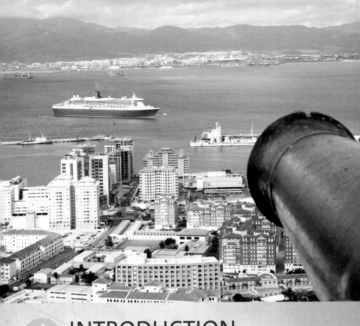

INTRODUCTION
Getting to know Gibraltar & the surrounding area

Getting to know Gibraltar & the surrounding area

Perched at the tip of Europe and dominated by a soaring limestone peak, Gibraltar packs a lot into its very small footprint. At first glance, the Rock – as it is affectionately known – is an old-fashioned British seaside resort given a sunny Mediterranean makeover. Tapas bars jostle for space with pubs and fish and chip restaurants, and narrow streets of whitewashed houses nod to their British standing with painted Union flags. But the Spanish and British cultures are not the only ones competing here. The backstreets are filled with the scent of simmering tagines and shops are crammed with Moroccan dates, spices and flat leather slippers.

Away from the town, the Upper Rock Nature Reserve is home to Gibraltar's most famous residents, the monkeys, which are tame enough to jump on tourists' shoulders and bold enough to make off with their cameras. The reserve is also the access point for an impressive network of siege tunnels blasted through the Rock as lookout points, as well as historic fortifications pitted by centuries-old cannon fire, and impressive natural caves, thick with stalagmites and stalactites, which are easily accessible and regularly used to stage concerts. The top of the Rock also affords unmissable views both to Spain and across the Strait of Gibraltar to Morocco.

Gibraltar is the ideal base for exploring both these places. The Costa del Sol's glamorous holiday playgrounds of Marbella and Puerto Banús are within easy reach, and the historic city of Ronda is close enough to make a satisfying day trip. Stretching to the west, the Costa de la Luz offers a more bohemian beach holiday, especially the kite-surfing mecca of Tarifa.

When the skies are clear here, you can see across the Straits so clearly that you can make out the individual houses in Morocco – which is of course the other great allure of holidaying in Gibraltar. The colourful souks of Tangier are a quick ferry hop away, making a rewarding target for a day trip, or the ideal springboard for exploration further afield.

⬤ *Looking past the tip of the Rock towards the Spanish coast*

THE BEST OF GIBRALTAR & THE SURROUNDING AREA

The Rock is the perfect base from which to explore a diverse range of places.

TOP 10 ATTRACTIONS

- **The Apes' Den** is home of the Rock's famous Barbary macaques – the only wild primates remaining in Europe (see pages 17–18).

- **Great Siege Tunnels** are a vast network of tunnels blasted through by British forces, which helped them triumph in the Great Siege of 1782 (see pages 20–21).

- **Upper Rock Nature Reserve** offers staggering views across the Straits to the Riff Mountains in Morocco, and is a paradise for bird lovers (see page 17).

- **Lazing on beaches** is easy. Pick one of Gibraltar's sandy coves, or head up the coast for the busy resorts of the Costa del Sol or the windswept strands of the Costa de la Luz (see pages 16–17).

- **St Michael's Cave** is the entry point to a remarkable network of caves inside the Rock. Take in the stunning stalactites and a concert in Upper St Michael Cave, or organise an unforgettable potholing trip deeper inside (see pages 22–3).

- **Wander around Marbella's *Casco Antiguo* (old town)**, with its picturesque main square, the Plaza de los Naranjos (see pages 43–9).

- **Tarifa** Watch kite-surfers during the day, then soak up the bohemian atmosphere of Tarifa's Moorish town centre over fresh mint *mojitos* or *caipirinhas* (see pages 66–7).

- **Grand Casemates Square** and Main Street are the heart of Gibraltar and the perfect places to mix tapas or a pub lunch with some people-watching (see page 20).

- **Ronda** is famous for its bullring, ancient bridge and amazing setting high above the River Guadalevin (see pages 78–81).

- **Lose yourself in the narrow streets of Tangier's medieval souk**, among Berber jewellery, woven rugs and bright earthenware tagines (see pages 73–7).

◐ *Beautiful illuminations in St Michael's Cave*

SYMBOLS KEY

The following symbols are used throughout this book:

ⓐ address ⓣ telephone ⓦ website address ⓔ email

ⓛ opening times ⓘ important

The following symbols are used on the maps:

i	information office	◯	city
✉	post office	◯	large town
⬛	shopping	◌	small town
✈	airport	◼	POI (point of interest)
➕	hospital	═	motorway
⛉	police station	—	main road
🚍	bus station	—	minor road
🚆	railway station	—	railway
✝	church		

❶ numbers denote featured cafés, restaurants & evening venues

RESTAURANT CATEGORIES

The symbol after the name of each restaurant listed in this guide indicates the price of a typical three-course meal without drinks for one person:

£ under £12 ££ £12–45 £££ more than £45

▶ *Gibraltar's beaches offer warm, clear waters and plenty of sun*

 RESORTS
Places under the sun

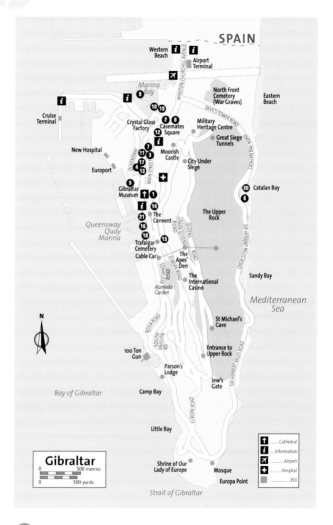

Gibraltar

SPAIN

Western Beach
Airport Terminal
Marina Bay
Cruise Terminal
North Front Cemetery (War Graves)
Eastern Beach
Crystal Glass Factory
Casemates Square
Military Heritage Centre
Great Siege Tunnels
New Hospital
Moorish Castle
City Under Siege
Europort
Gibraltar Museum
The Upper Rock
Catalan Bay
Queensway Quay Marina
The Convent
Trafalgar Cemetery
Cable Car
The Apes' Den
The International Casino
Mediterranean Sea
Sandy Bay
Alameda Garden
St Michael's Cave
100 Ton Gun
Entrance to Upper Rock
Parson's Lodge
Jew's Gate
Bay of Gibraltar
Camp Bay
Little Bay
Shrine of Our Lady of Europe
Mosque
Europa Point
Strait of Gibraltar

N

Gibraltar
0   500 metres
0   500 yards

Cathedral
Information
Airport
Hospital
POI

14

Gibraltar

Gibraltar – or 'Gib' as it is more colloquially known – is dominated by a soaring chunk of limestone that stands over 420 m (1,390 ft) high and guards the narrow entrance to the Mediterranean. This strategic position is also the key to its chequered past. The Rock was first inhabited by the Phoenicians, who used it as a landmark signalling the entrance to the Mediterranean, then by a variety of invaders and finally by the Moors. The Moorish leader Tarik gave it its present name, derived from *Gebel Tarik*, which means 'Tarik's Mountain' in Arabic.

Since then, Gibraltar has been repeatedly fought over by the Spanish and the British, who finally conquered the territory more than 300 years ago in 1704. Gibraltar is a melting pot of many different cultures but the one thing that unites the Jewish, Moroccan and Catholic populations is a fierce pride in the Gibraltarian national identity and heritage. Backstreets are decorated with Union flags; many older Gibraltarians refuse to cross the border into Spain; and every year 10 September is given over to a highly political 'national day' celebration, when the entire population of 30,000 turns out in the colours of the Gibraltar flag, red and white. One of the most common questions outsiders ask about Gibraltar's citizens is whether they are originally Spanish or English, but in truth many Gibraltarian families have been on the Rock for centuries, hailing from places like Malta and Genoa. They have British passports, Spanish sensibilities and, away from public functions, speak Llanito (pronounced *yaneeto*) – a confusing melée of Spanish and English with a few unique extra words thrown in for good measure.

Gibraltarians embrace tourists of all nationalities and are keen to make sure they enjoy their stay on the Rock. However, those who spend more than a few days on the Rock are almost certain to find themselves in a political discussion and they would be well advised to tread carefully. Gibraltarians voted 97 per cent in favour of remaining British at the last referendum and do not respond well to outsiders suggesting they should surrender their sovereignty.

Certainly, Gibraltar is very like a British town to look at. The street furniture, signposts, phone boxes, food, currency and pubs are all British – but the climate and the beaches are decidedly Mediterranean, making it a popular destination for British expats. It is also an ideal place for a shopping spree, with sizeable discounts available on jewellery, cosmetics, alcohol and Lladro porcelain because of its VAT-free status.

But the real joys of Gibraltar are to be discovered away from the main town, in the backstreets dotted with magnificent colonial buildings and Moroccan corner shops selling fat dates and leather slippers. And then there is the Upper Rock Nature Reserve, which affords access to the Rock's most famous residents – the monkeys – as well as historical sights and unbeatable views over the Straits.

You need to show your passport on entering and leaving Gibraltar. Border formalities are less protracted than they used to be, but motorists may be better off parking in La Linea on the Spanish side. On Sundays, many of the shops and sights are closed, unless a cruise ship is in port.

BEACHES

Gibraltar's beaches combine sunshine and warm, clear waters with the beach umbrella culture of a British seaside town. Be warned: they can get busy in the summer months.

Catalan Bay, a sandy cove also known as Caleta, is the best choice for families. It is located next to a village of the same name at the base of the steep east side of the Rock, which casts the beach in shadow by around 18.00, and is relatively sheltered for swimming. Nearby there is parking as well as a number of decent fish restaurants to choose from.

Eastern Beach is Gibraltar's biggest beach and the most popular with teens and 20-somethings. Like Catalan Bay it faces east but it does not sit in the shadow of the Rock so is a great place to enjoy the evening sun. A *chiringuito* (snack hut) opens on the beach during the summer.

Sandy Bay is also popular with young families, who make the most of a playground and saltwater swimming pool. It is a favourite launch point for shore divers and good for snorkelling too.

Western Beach is a tiny beach by the airport and has declined in recent years (*E. coli* was found there in late 2010). However, it remains popular with office workers as it gets the last of the evening sun.

THINGS TO SEE & DO

Upper Rock Nature Reserve
A blanket charge is made to enter any part of the Reserve, which includes many of Gibraltar's chief attractions (including the Great Siege Tunnels, the Mediterranean Steps, the Moorish Castle and St Michael's Cave) but is well worth a visit in its own right for the stunning views across the Straits to the Riff Mountains in Morocco. It is also a paradise for bird lovers: more than 200 migratory species have been spotted here.
🕐 09.30–19.15 (summer); 09.30–17.30 (winter)

Alameda Garden
Located just south of the city walls, the Alameda Garden hosts an impressive collection of plants from Mediterranean climatic zones around the world and is also used as a research outpost for well-known botanic centres like Kew Gardens in the UK. It is sometimes referred to as 'Alameda Wildlife Park' – a name that sets up false expectations – but as long as you are not expecting a safari it is well worth a visit. It also features an open-air theatre, which is used for weddings as well as concerts and the annual Miss Gibraltar beauty pageant.
🅐 Red Sands Road 📞 200 41235 🅦 www.gibraltargardens.gi
🕐 08.00–sunset daily

The Apes' Den
Halfway up the Rock are the famous Barbary macaques. Although they are wild, they are bold enough to climb on tourists and have been known

MONKEYING AROUND

Mention the name Gibraltar, and most people think of monkeys. Despite the 'Apes' Den' signs, the Barbary macaques are a type of tailless monkey and the only group of wild primates remaining in Europe. They are thought to have originally migrated to Gibraltar from the Atlas Mountains in Morocco, although how is unclear, and former British prime minister Winston Churchill famously solidified their link with the Rock by declaring that Gibraltar would remain British as long as the monkeys remained there.

But for locals they represent as much of a nuisance as a blessing. Some of the packs regularly descend into town and cause mayhem by raiding dustbins and stealing food. They also have a nasty bite and injured tourists are admitted to casualty on a daily basis.

However, people who do not feed or try to touch the monkeys should not encounter any problems. Although the monkeys are wild, they are cared for by the Gibraltar Ornithology and Natural History Society (GONHS), which scatters a balanced diet of seeds and raw fruit in the undergrowth at the top of the Rock in order to encourage the monkeys to scavenge. GONHS also keeps track of each specimen by mapping their freckles and dental records so that it can administer contraceptive injections and carefully control pack politics and size.

to make off with cameras etc, so hang on carefully to your belongings. Don't feed them, even if your taxi driver encourages you to.

ⓐ Upper Rock Nature Reserve ⓣ 200 74950 (Gibraltar Tourist Board)
ⓛ 09.30–19.15 daily (summer); 09.30–17.30 daily (winter)

Cable Car

Enjoy spectacular views as you climb to the top of the Rock in this eight-minute cable-car journey. Cars leave every 15 minutes and under-threes go free.

ⓐ Grand Parade ⓣ 200 77826 ⓛ 09.30–19.15 daily

The Convent

One of Gibraltar's oldest buildings, the Convent was founded as a Franciscan friary in 1531 and became the official residence of the Governor of Gibraltar in 1728. It is not accessible to the public, but visitors can still enjoy the Royal Gibraltar Regiment's changing of the guard ceremony, which takes place outside several times a day on weekdays. Military history buffs will also appreciate the brass cannons.

Dolphin watching

Watch the three species of dolphin that swim in the bay from a specially designed glass-bottom boat. There are occasional sightings of pilot whales too. Reliable excursions are organised year-round through:

Dolphin Adventure ⓐ Marina Bay ⓣ 200 50650 or 685 60 82 08 ⓦ www.dolphinadventure.eu

Dolphin World ⓐ Ferry Terminal, Waterport ⓣ 677 27 88 45

The Original Dolphin Safari ⓐ 6 The Square, Marina Bay ⓣ 200 71914 or 607 29 04 00 ⓦ www.dolphinsafari.gi

Europa Point

On a clear day, you can see all the way to Africa from the southernmost point of the Rock – the 'tip of Europe'. It is also the site of the impressive King Fahd bin Abdulaziz al-Saud Mosque – one of the biggest mosques in Europe.

Gibraltar Crystal Glass Factory

See traditional glass-blowing in action in this museum and shop, without any pressure to buy.

ⓐ Grand Casemates Square ⓛ 09.00–19.00 Mon–Fri, 09.00–14.00 Sat, closed Sun

The Gibraltar Museum and Moorish Baths

A visit to Gibraltar's museum provides an invaluable historic insight into the Rock, including artefacts from Phoenician and Neanderthal settlements as well as its more recent past, and a 15-minute film

summarising its history. The lower part of the museum also houses what's claimed to be the best-preserved Moorish bathhouse in Europe.
ⓐ 18/20 Bomb House Lane ⓣ 200 74289 ⓦ www.gib.gi/museum
ⓛ 10.00–18.00 Mon–Fri, 10.00–14.00 Sat, closed Sun ⓘ Admission charge

Grand Casemates Square

Casemates, as this large plaza is colloquially known, is the social hub of Gibraltar. Lined with restaurants and bars spilling into the main square, it is the place to mix people-watching with pub grub, tapas and fish and chips by day, and to enjoy drinks flowing at night. Many of the bars host live music in the evenings, and during the summer the square itself is used to stage performances by local musicians.

Great Siege Tunnels

This vast network of tunnels (48 km/29 miles long) was blasted into the Rock in 1782 so that British forces could position their cannons at a great

● *One of the re-created scenes in the Great Siege Tunnels*

height and win the Great Siege. An interesting exhibition shows what it would have been like to be a soldier during the campaign.

ⓐ Hay's Level, Upper Rock ⏱ 10.30–17.30 Mon–Sat, closed Sun

Kings Bastion Leisure Centre

This modern leisure centre is perfect for rainy days. It offers a two-screen cinema, a 14-lane bowling alley, a small ice rink, and arcade games in a light and airy complex that has been impressively designed to incorporate the city walls it takes its name from. The centre also hosts under-18 discos and its Rock Bastion Café is a useful spot for a snack.

ⓐ Queensway ☎ 200 44777 ⓦ www.kingsbastion.gov.gi
⏱ 10.00–24.00 daily

Mediterranean Steps

This demanding walk takes you from Jew's Gate (the entrance to the Upper Rock) up to the very top of the Rock, along its southern façade. The steps are poorly maintained, so only attempt this if you are sure-footed and have good grip on your shoes. It's well worth the effort, though, especially on a clear day when the views across the Straits are incredible.

ⓐ Upper Rock Nature Reserve ☎ 200 74950 (Gibraltar Tourist Board)
⏱ 09.30–19.15 daily (summer); 09.30–17.30 daily (winter)

Moorish Castle

Only the Tower of Homage remains of this 8th-century castle, which was erected by Abu'l Hassan when the Moors seized Gibraltar. It was later used by Gibraltarians to take refuge from marauding Turkish pirates who virtually destroyed the town, and remains pockmarked with the cannonball scars of various sieges. The lower castle formerly stretched all the way down to Grand Casemates Square in the town centre. It was used as a prison for many years, but was being refurbished as a tourist destination at the time of research.

ⓐ Upper Rock Nature Reserve ☎ 200 74950 (Gibraltar Tourist Board)
⏱ 09.30–19.15 daily (summer); 09.30–17.30 daily (winter)

⬥ *The rock formations in St Michael's Cave*

Ocean Village

Built in 2009, this luxury development in Marina Bay is a relatively new addition to Gibraltar and has provided Casemates with some serious competition as the centre of social activity. Its seafront bars and restaurants are pricier than others in Gibraltar, but are the ideal place to wind down with a drink and a good meal, or to get started on a lively night out. Familiar names like Pizza Express jostle with popular local establishments like Savannah, which regularly invites major international DJs to perform. There is also a casino and a range of shops.

St Michael's Cave

Filled with stalactites and stalagmites, St Michael's Cave is the largest of the group of caves on Gibraltar, and has played a fundamental role in its chequered history. It was once home to groups of Neolithic people, then used as a hospital during World War II, and now functions as a dramatic backdrop to concerts and fashion shows. Legend has it that there is an underground tunnel from one of the caves that leads under the Straits to Africa. The concreted floor of Upper St Michael's Cave detracts from the magical feel but makes it easy to access, even with pushchairs and wheelchairs. Visit as part of a daytime tour of the Upper Rock, or attend one of the regular evening concerts. Check the *Gibraltar Chronicle* and posters in local cafés for details.

Evening caving trips to Lower St Michael's Cave can also be organised through the Gibraltar Tourist Board with at least three days' notice. The three-hour excursion is challenging, but well worth the effort for the chance to experience Gibraltar's unspoilt stalactite formations and its beautiful underground lake.

ⓐ Upper Rock Nature Reserve ⓣ 200 74950 (Gibraltar Tourist Board)

Scuba diving

The sheltered Bay of Gibraltar is a good place for beginners, and also has the added attractions of an artificial reef rich in sea life and a whole host of sunken wrecks to explore. Useful contacts include:

Dive Charters ⓐ 4 Admiral's Walk, Marina Bay ⓣ 200 45649
ⓦ www.divegib.gi
Dive Hire Naui Centre ⓐ 36 B/C Waterport Circle, Sheppard's Marina
ⓣ 200 73616 ⓦ www.divehire.co.uk
Rock Marine ⓐ The Square, Marina Bay ⓣ 200 73147

Trafalgar Cemetery

This small graveyard just south of the city walls was used as Gibraltar's military cemetery in the early 19th century, and is the final resting place of two soldiers who died in the Battle of Trafalgar (1805), which famously took place in the Bay of Gibraltar. A ceremony is held here every Trafalgar Day (21 October) to commemorate Lord Nelson's victory.

TAKING A BREAK

Gibraltar Arms £ ❶ English-style pub serving up steak and kidney pie and other traditional pub dishes, all at very reasonable prices. Pints and

free Wi-Fi are also available. ⓐ 184 Main Street ⓣ 200 72133
ⓦ www.gibraltararms.gi ⓛ 07.30–late Mon–Sat, 09.30–late Sun

Latino's & Latino's on the Beach £ ❷ One of the most popular
restaurants on Grand Casemates Square, with another *chiringuito*-style
branch right on Eastern Beach. The menu offers nachos, sandwiches,
chilli con carne and hearty salads. ⓐ Grand Casemates Square/Eastern
Beach ⓣ 200 47755 (Latino's) or 200 43555 (Latino's on the Beach)
ⓦ www.latinosrestaurants.com

Maharaja £ ❸ Friendly, low-key Indian restaurant and the best place
to sample Britain's official favourite dish – chicken tikka masala.
ⓐ 5 Tuckey's Lane ⓣ 200 75233 ⓛ 10.00–16.00, 19.00–20.00 daily

Pizzaghetti Factory £ ❹ Super-friendly Italian restaurant offering tasty
pizza and pasta dishes at pocket-friendly prices – that become dirt cheap
if you order to take away. It also serves continental breakfasts. ⓐ 56/58
Irish Town ⓣ 200 70808 ⓛ 08.00–24.00 Mon–Sat, closed Sun

Rock Bastian Café £ ❺ This friendly café inside the Kings Bastion
Leisure Centre offers a decent range of generously portioned snacks,
including nachos and fast-food platters to share. ⓐ Kings Bastion Leisure
Centre, Queensway ⓣ 200 52442 ⓛ 10.00–22.00 daily

Seawave Fish Restaurant £ ❻ Super-casual fish restaurant in
Catalan Bay. Avoid the blaring television inside, and enjoy your *raciones*
(portions) of freshly caught cod, *calamares* and *gambas al pil-pil*
overlooking the sea. Just watch out for the seagulls. ⓐ 60 Catalan Bay
Village ⓣ 200 78739

The Star Bar £ ❼ Reputedly the oldest pub on the Rock, this friendly
little bar just off Main Street is as good a place as any to sample a
traditional English fry-up or fish and chips in the sun. ⓐ Parliament Lane
ⓣ 200 75924 ⓛ 07.30–00.30 Mon–Sat, 10.30–00.30 Sun

⬥ *Dine somewhere with a sea view to enjoy the sunset over the Mediterranean*

All's Well ££ ❽   One of a number of bars built inside the historical artillery stores off Grand Casemates Square, All's Well has the feel of a traditional English pub and is popular throughout the day and evening. ⓐ 4 Grand Casemates Square ❶ 200 72987 ⓛ 11.00–01.00 daily

Bianca's ££ ❾   Relaxed restaurant overlooking the marina, good for nachos and sangria or a full-blown dinner. All the usual pizzas, meat and fish dishes, as well as a few surprises like banana pizza and steak stuffed with prawns. ⓐ 6/7 Admiral's Walk ❶ 200 73379 ⓛ 09.00–late daily

A Garota de Ipanema ££ ❿   Lively Brazilian bar and *churrascaria*. Pay a set price and eat all you want from the buffet or from the *pasadors* – staff carrying skewers stacked with freshly cooked meat. ⓐ 11 Ocean Village Promenade ❶ 216 48888 ⓛ 12.00–16.00, 19.00–23.00 Mon–Fri, 19.00–23.00 Sat, 12.00–17.00 Sun

Café Rojo ££ ⓫   Hearty sandwiches and inventive salads, like smoked duck with papaya. The evening menu also offers hot dishes ranging from lamb shoulder to poached salmon. ⓐ 54 Irish Town ❶ 200 51738 ⓛ From 10.00–late Mon–Fri, closed Sat lunch & Sun

Café Solo ££ ⓬   Popular restaurant on the plaza serving modern European dishes with an Italian bias. Excellent duck as well as salads, pastas and pizzas. ⓐ Grand Casemates Square ❶ 200 44449 ⓛ Breakfast and dinner

The Clipper ££ ⓭   Hearty pub grub and Sunday roasts in a lively atmosphere. International sports events shown on big-screen TVs. ⓐ 78b Irish Town ❶ 200 79791 ⓛ 09.30–24.00 daily

Latino's Diner ££ ⓮   Part of the Latino's chain, but with a very different feel to its sister-restaurants, this two-storey establishment opposite Gibraltar Cathedral serves up classic American fare.

Hamburgers, milkshakes and fries are on the menu alongside fried chicken and sizzling steaks. **a** 194–196 Main Street **t** 200 46660 **l** 09.00–19.00 daily

Marrakesh Restaurant ££ **15** Tucked away on a quiet square behind the main drag, this is the best spot in Gibraltar for tasty couscous and hearty tagines. After lunch, explore the streets nearby for Moroccan slippers and earthenware. **a** 7 Governor's Parade **t** 200 75196 **l** 12.00–23.00 Mon–Sat, closed Sun

14 On The Quay ££ **16** Situated in Gibraltar's quietest marina, this waterside restaurant is a little old-fashioned but offers a good range of elaborate meat and fish dishes. **a** 14 Queensway Quay Marina **t** 200 43731 **l** 12.30–23.00 daily

Sacarello Coffee & Co ££ **17** This Gibraltarian institution offers light lunches as well as good coffee and delicious home-made quiches and cakes. The interior is decorated with local art, which is for sale. It is also a good place to check what events are going on locally. **a** 57 Irish Town **t** 200 70625 **l** 09.00–19.30 Mon–Fri, 09.00–15.00 Sat, closed Sun

Casa Pepe £££ **18** Traditional waterfront tapas bar serving delicious Spanish specialities like paella, as well as Argentinian beef. The only drawback is the prices, which are on a par with those in Britain. **a** 18 Queensway Quay Marina **t** 200 46967 **l** 12.00–16.00, 19.00–late Mon–Fri, Sat 19.00 onwards, closed Sun

Gauchos £££ **19** This small restaurant just through a tunnel from Casemates offers delicious Argentinian dishes like *chorizo criolla* (spicy barbecued sausage) and grilled cheese. **a** Waterport Casemates **t** 200 59700 **l** 19.30–23.00 Mon–Sat, closed Sun

La Mamela £££ **20** Upmarket fish restaurant in Gibraltar's 'fishing village'. Eat inside or on the terrace, which has attractive sea views.

⊚ Catalan Bay ☎ 200 50540 🕑 12.30–15.00, 20.00–23.00 Mon–Sat, 12.00–15.00 Sun

Waterfront £££ ㉑ Reliable restaurant overlooking Gibraltar's smartest marina, and serving a range of international cuisine from Indian curries to steak and kidney pie. Wi-Fi access is also available. ⊚ Queensway Quay Marina ☎ 200 45666 ⓦ www.waterfront.co.gi 🕑 From 09.00 daily

AFTER DARK

Restaurants
Corks Wine Bar £ Don't be fooled by the name – Corks stands out as much as a place to eat as it does to drink. A combination of good-quality pub food, pleasant décor and attentive staff make it a popular stop for business lunches. It also serves ice cream and decent coffee in the airy parlour at the front. There is live music on Thursdays. ⊚ 79 Irish Town ☎ 200 75566 🕑 08.30–late Mon–Sat, closed Sun

Salsa Fuego ££ By day this modern-looking establishment is a decent restaurant specialising in hearty meat dishes, but it really comes into its own at 23.00 when tables are cleared away to make room for live music. ⊚ 12 Grand Casemates Square ☎ 200 43111 🕑 11.00–03.00 daily

Savannah ££ This restaurant-cum-bar is relatively pricey by Gibraltarian standards but is hugely popular nonetheless, not least for its waterside location. Enjoy a relaxed drink on one of its outside sofas, or let your hair down to one of the big-name DJs who frequently fly in for an evening on the decks. ⊚ Leisure Island, Ocean Village ☎ 200 66666 ⓦ www.savannah.gi

Nightlife
Celebrity Wine Bar Relaxed waterside bar serving a well-heeled crowd. Particularly good for cocktails. ⊚ Sail 3.2 Ocean Village Marina ☎ 200 40972 🕑 11.00–01.00 daily

Lord Nelson This bar is slightly more expensive and lower key than some of its Casemates neighbours, but is well suited to those nights when you want to hear yourself over the music … unless you go on a Saturday when it hosts a live band. ⓐ 10 Grand Casemates Square ⓣ 200 50009 ⓛ 10.00–01.00 daily

The O'Callaghan Eliott Hotel Hosts a popular jazz night every Thursday and some Sundays, with talented visiting musicians. Ask or check the *Gibraltar Chronicle* for details. ⓐ 2 Governor's Parade ⓣ 200 70500

The Three Owls This discreet bar is neither the nicest nor the cheapest in Gibraltar, but it has become something of an institution because it tends to stay open on quiet evenings when rivals shut up shop. It also has a pool table. ⓐ 102 Irish Town ⓣ 200 77446 ⓛ 10.30–01.30 daily

The Tunnel A Casemates stalwart, this lively bar stays busy into the early hours and hosts karaoke on Wednesdays. ⓔ 8 Grand Casemates Square ⓣ 200 74946 ⓛ 11.00–late daily

Vibes Up some stairs just off Grand Casemates Square, this small disco is the place to go when things quieten down elsewhere. Expect a mix of UK chart and Spanish summer anthems. ⓐ Linewall Road ⓛ Closed Sun

◓ The marina at Estepona

Estepona

The beachfront resort of Estepona is quietly becoming one of the most fashionable places on the western Costas. Its pleasure marina is making glamorous Puerto Banús look to its laurels, while its golf courses attract many well-known international faces. Estepona, though, caters better for young families than the jet set. It makes no sightseeing demands on visitors, but there are few more relaxing places for a stroll than its tidy, palm-lined esplanades. For a drink and a good meal, head for the cafés and restaurants around the jasmine-scented Plaza de las Flores.

This modest, low-rise town spreads along a large expanse of beach. Its economic mainstays once revolved around fishing and citrus growing – the streets in the old quarter all have charming, ceramic name plaques decorated with lemons. Unlike some parts of the Costas, agriculture and fishing have not entirely given way to the demands of tourism, and the town still has an unpretentious and refreshingly Spanish air. Estepona's harbour is a hive of activity when the night's catch is landed on the quaysides. If you get up very early, the fish market by the Puerto Pesquero is a sight to see, but it's mostly over by 07.00. The quiet, flattish coastline is guarded by ancient fortresses, some dating from Roman or Phoenician times. Some distance inland, the road through the Serranía Bermeja climbs through forests where a unique species of fir tree called the *pinsapo* flourishes. From the Refugio de los Reales *mirador* (viewing point), spectacular views extend as far as Gibraltar.

BEACHES

Estepona manages a 21-km (13-mile) stretch of coastline, and proudly waves a Blue Flag (the EU's quality stamp) on several of its beaches. The main strand is the long, sandy **Playa de la Rada**, punctuated by *chiringuitos* (beach bars) and the wooden watchtowers of the lifeguards. **Playa del Cristo**, near the marina, is a delightful oyster-shaped cove of sheltered, gently shelving sand, ideal for children. If you prefer life in the buff, head eastwards for the **Costa Natura**, Spain's oldest naturist resort.

THINGS TO SEE & DO

Golf

Estepona has five local golf courses and several championship links around the smart *urbanización* of Sotogrande. The superb **Valderrama** course rose to fame when it hosted the Ryder Cup in 1997.

ⓐ 11310 Sotogrande ⓣ 956 79 12 00 ⓦ www.valderrama.com

Polo

For polo, head for Sotogrande, near Estepona, where British and Argentinian teams practise their chukkas during the winter, on Spain's only permanent polo field. Tuition available.

ⓐ Santa María Polo ⓣ 956 61 00 12 ⓦ www.santamariapoloclub.com

Selwo Safari Park

A successful safari park with over 2,000 exotic species, from giraffes to panthers, in their natural habitat. There are also daily shows.

ⓐ Carretera N340, Km 162.5 ⓣ 902 19 04 82 ⓦ www.selwo.es
ⓒ 10.00–18.00 daily ⓘ Admission charge

TAKING A BREAK

La Gamba £ Simple seafood tapas bar, with fish and some meats.
ⓐ Calle Terraza 25 ⓣ 952 80 56 07 ⓒ Closed Thur & 15 Feb–15 Mar

Gelateria Caffè del Centro £ Coffee, sandwiches and delicious Italian ice creams served in a pretty square with a fountain. ⓐ Plaza Doctor 1
ⓣ 952 80 55 96 ⓒ 11.00–03.00 daily

Los Pinchitos £ Low-key tapas bar specialising in skewered meats.
ⓐ Mariana Pirieda 8 ⓣ 952 80 08 29 ⓒ 18.00–late daily

Chiringuito Rossi ££ This family-friendly *chiringuito* (beach bar) is suitable for a quick snack or a full-blown meal. Great beach views all the

◐ *A fishing boat returning to Estepona*

way to Gibraltar. ⓐ Paseo Marítimo, opposite Plaza Ortiz ❶ 952 11 32 99
🕒 Mar–Oct

AFTER DARK

Restaurants
Casa de Mi Abuela ££ Rustic décor and hearty platters of Argentinian-style chargrilled meat. ⓐ Calle Caridad 54 ❶ 952 79 19 67 🕒 Closed Tues & May

El Rincon Toscano ££ Smart Italian restaurant with a wide variety of fish, meat and pasta dishes. ⓐ Calle Real 22–26 ❶ 952 79 59 14 🕒 Closed Wed & Feb & Nov

Marisquería El Gavilán del Mar £££ Great seafood restaurant in one of the old town's prettiest plazas. ⓐ Plaza Doctor Arce ❶ 952 80 28 56 🕒 Closed Tues, and Mon in winter

San Pedro de Alcántara

West of Marbella, the little town of San Pedro de Alcántara nestles on a broad strip of fertile, coastal lowland sheltered by rugged hills. It is less well known than its glitzy neighbours, but Costa del Sol experts recognise a good thing when they see it and many expatriates have chosen to settle here.

San Pedro dates from the 1860s, when it was established as a model farming community with an agricultural training school. Today, many of its country estates are prosperous tourist enclaves or golf courses. Much of the town lies inland behind the coastal highway, and it's a fair step down to the beach.

There's less nightlife here than in Marbella or Puerto Banús, but its plus points include a well-managed stretch of quiet, clean seafront and three of the most interesting archaeological remains anywhere on the coast. The charming old town centres on the shady Avenida Marqués del Duero, lined with enticing shops and cafés, orange trees and fountains.

BEACHES

There are fantastic watersports facilities at **Bora-Bora Beach**, including waterskiing, motorboats, canoes, rowing boats, as well as scuba diving.
ⓐ Urbanización Lindavista, Calle Gitanilla

SHOPPING
Street Market Every Thursday there's a lively market near the Sports Pavilion, for those with an eye for a bargain.
Vassiliki This is a popular backwater for local artists. For postcards, pottery, jewellery, ceramics and unique examples of local art, head for the shop called Katoi. ⓐ On the Ponti road, next door to Mythos Taverna ☏ 264 50 31 700

THINGS TO SEE & DO

Archaeological remains

Behind the beach at Las Bovedas lies a Roman bathhouse with a wood-fired heating system, and a 4th-century basilica with a beautiful font. Four kilometres (2½ miles) east at Río Verde is a Roman villa decorated with delightful mosaics showing kitchen utensils.
🕔 952 78 13 60 🕓 Free guided tours on Tues, Thur & Sat at 12.00.
Meet at the tourist office inside the archway which signposts entry into San Pedro and Marbella, on the Carretera N340, Km 170.5

⬥ San Pedro de Alcántara's pretty church

Cable skiing

Perfect your waterskiing skills on a calm lake, towed along a fixed overhead wire – easier than an erratic, fast-moving boat.
Cable Ski Marbella ⓐ Parque de las Medranas ⓣ 952 78 55 79
ⓦ www.cableskimarbella.es ⓛ 11.00–15.00, 16.00–21.00 daily

Riding

Call a day ahead to book a horse trek through the countryside at
Lakeview Equestrian Centre.
ⓐ Urbanización Valle del Sol ⓣ 952 78 69 34 ⓛ Tues–Sun, closed Mon

TAKING A BREAK

La Pesquera de San Pedro ££ Enjoy sardines barbecued on the seafront or prawns *pil-pil* (in sizzling oil with garlic and chilli) at the local branch of this chain of family-friendly fish restaurants. ⓐ Avenida del Mediterráneo, Playa San Pedro de Alcántara ⓣ 952 78 77 21

AFTER DARK

Restaurants

Caruso ££ Smart, modern restaurant serving popular dishes and adventurous daily specials. ⓐ Calle Andalucía, Local 6 ⓣ 952 78 22 93
ⓛ Dinner only, 19.30–24.00 Mon–Sat, closed Sun

El Gamonal ££ Some of the best cooking around, in a flower-filled, country setting off the Ronda road. Specialises in roasts and whole fish baked in salt. ⓐ Camino La Quinta ⓣ 952 78 99 21 ⓛ Closed Wed & mid-Jan–mid-Feb

Mesón El Coto £££ Lovely terrace restaurant high in the hills on the road to Ronda. Attentive service and excellent country dishes and game.
ⓐ Urbanización el Madroñal, Carretera de Ronda ⓣ 952 78 66 01
ⓛ 19.30–00.30 daily

Puerto Banús

Marbella's exclusive and world-famous marina – Puerto Banús – just a short distance to the west, is the playground of the rich and famous, where the international jet set come to shop, socialise and party. It is the Costa del Sol's most celebrated port, filled with a dazzling collection of massive, ostentatious yachts and gin palaces operated by battalions of uniformed crew – very much the place to see and be seen. Behind the port, the 'Golden Mile' to Marbella throbs with nightspots and restaurants. Spot King Fahd's exotic Arabian palace, Mar Mar. Inland, the glitterati villas and exclusive country clubs of Nueva Andalucía stretch back into the hills.

This glamorous complex, named after its designer José Banús, was created in 1968, and its success has spawned a number of rival wannabes up and down the coast. Few, though, can boast the spectacular backdrop of rugged hills, which gives the marina its photogenic setting. A village-like development of eye-catching, pantiled apartments in Spanish and Moorish styles surrounds the waterfront walkways, forming a seamless chain of eating places, bars and boutiques. As the sun sinks below the yardarm, beautiful people strut their stuff on the quaysides before leisurely making their way to the most fashionable nightlife venues.

THINGS TO SEE & DO

Aquarium Puerto Banús

A fascinating place for all the family, this aquarium is housed in an old watchtower at the port.

ⓐ Torre de control ☎ 952 81 87 67 🕒 10.00–13.30, 16.30–19.30 Mon–Sat, closed Sun

Golf

No dedicated golfer should miss out on a visit to the **Marbella Golf and Country Club** (see page 45).

◒ *Flowers and boats in Puerto Banús Marina*

SHOPPING

La Cañada Enormous out-of-town shopping mall off the N340 to Marbella, with multi-screen cinema and all the major Spanish high-street stores. 🕐 10.00–22.00 Mon–Sat, closed Sun

El Corte Inglés This massive department store and supermarket stocks just about everything. 🅰 Ramón Areces, Centro Comercial Costa Marbella, on the outskirts of Puerto Banús 🕽 952 90 99 90 🆆 www.elcorteingles.es 🕐 Closed Sun (winter)

Craft market Ideal place to browse for jewellery, bohemian beachwear and *objets d'art*, under white tents in the main square.

Market A large fleamarket. 🅰 Held around the bullring of Nueva Andalucía 🕐 09.00–14.00 Sat

AFTER DARK

Restaurants

Azul Marino ££ Superb international cuisine served in a smart restaurant with nautical décor in a magnificent prime waterfront location. 🅰 Muelle Ribera 🕽 952 81 10 44 🆆 www.buenas-mesas.com 🕐 12.00–01.00 daily

Dalli's Pizza and Pasta Factory ££ Pizza and pasta combined in this cheerful Italian restaurant, with an adjoining café. 🅰 Avenida Fontanilla 🕽 952 81 86 23 🕐 19.00–01.00 daily

El Rancho del Puerto ££ Suckling pig and other tasty meats are on offer in this steakhouse. 🅰 Muelle Benabola 4 🕽 952 81 62 52

Red Pepper ££ Friendly Greek restaurant right on the quayside. 🅰 Muelle Ribera 🕽 952 81 21 48 🕐 11.00–01.00 daily

Finca Besaya £££ This exclusive, relaxing hideaway is situated in an old avocado farm nestled high in the hills. Accomplished cooking.

⬤ *Fashionable Puerto Banús is fantastic for glamorous shopping*

ⓐ Urbanización Río Verde Alto ⓣ 952 86 13 82 ⓛ 19.30–24.00 Tues–Sun, closed Mon ⓘ Booking essential; dress smartly

Restaurante Antonio £££ Elegant corner restaurant specialising in seafood, but also offering an extensive selection of delicious meat dishes. ⓐ Muelle Ribera 21 ⓣ 952 81 35 36 ⓛ 13.00–16.00, 19.30–23.00 daily ⓘ Booking essential

Nightlife
Stereo Lounge ££ Modern, chilled-out bar with comfy sofas and a marina view. ⓐ Muelle Ribera 18

Olivia Valére £££ Celebrated nightclub, and haunt of the rich and famous. Smart restaurant, sushi and piano bars. ⓐ Carretera de Istán, Km 0.8, Nueva Andalucía ⓣ 952 82 88 61 ⓦ www.oliviavalere.com ⓛ Restaurant 21.00–01.00; nightclub 24.00–05.00 daily

Sinatra Bar £££ Rub shoulders with the likes of Antonio Banderas in this laid-back, see-and-be-seen, waterfront bar. ⓐ Muelle Ribera 2 ⓣ 952 81 90 50

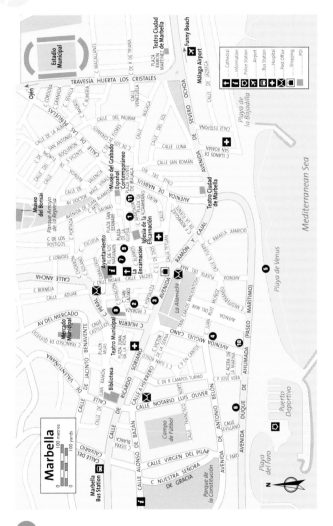

Marbella

Glamorous and cosmopolitan yet fiercely traditional, Marbella perfectly blends old with new and is considered by many to be the jewel of the resorts along the Costa del Sol.

The old town (*Casco Antiguo*) has been carefully and sympathetically maintained – a quaint pedestrian district of tiny squares and white-washed houses smothered in bougainvillea clusters round the postcard-pretty Plaza de los Naranjos, named after its orange trees. By contrast, modern Marbella centres around its designer-boutique-lined Avenida Ricardo de Soviano, and the seafront. In the evenings, its smart promenade becomes a catwalk for well-dressed Spanish families.

BEACHES & WATERSPORTS

The Marbella coastline has 26 km (16 miles) of attractive, well-tended sandy beaches. The central beaches stretch either side of the *puerto deportivo* (yacht marina) below elegant, traffic-free promenades. There are plenty of places to lounge beneath a parasol, but many visitors seize the opportunity to enjoy energetic, high-tech watersports of all kinds.

Club Marítimo de Marbella Scuba diving, sailing and windsurfing near Marbella's yacht harbour. ⓐ Puerto Deportivo ⓣ 952 77 25 04

Happy Divers Marbella Scuba diving and boat trips. ⓐ Puerto Deportivo 52 ⓣ 952 88 36 17 ⓦ www.happy-divers-marbella.com

Hotel Marbella Club Motorboats, windsurfing, kite-surfing, waterskiing, pedalos, canoes and catamarans. ⓐ Blvd Príncipe Alfonso von Hohenlohe ⓣ 952 82 22 11

Hotel Puente Romano Motorboats, windsurfing, kite-surfing, waterskiing, pedalos, canoes and catamarans. ⓐ Carretera N340, Km 177 ⓣ 952 82 09 00 ⓦ www.puenteromano.com

◔ The breathtaking setting of the Aloha Golf course

THINGS TO SEE & DO

Funny Beach

Go-karting, laser games, water slides, bumper boats (an aquatic version of dodgems), mini-golf, jet-skiing and a giant Scalextric.
ⓐ Carretera N340, Km 184 ❶ 952 82 33 59 Ⓦ www.funnybeach.com

Golf

For anyone interested in golf there are many splendid courses in the area immediately around Marbella. So high is the standard of the golfing facilities that numerous top international players come here to practise during the winter, and some have permanent connections with the area. The swankiest clubs are situated mostly to the west in the hills of Nueva Andalucía. Most demand a handicap certificate, and require booking well in advance. Contact the tourist office for details.
Aloha Golf ⓐ Nueva Andalucía Ⓦ www.clubdegolfaloha.com
Marbella Golf and Country Club This exclusive course is on the Málaga side. ⓐ Carretera N340, Km 188 ❶ 952 83 05 00 Ⓦ www.marbellagolf.com
La Quinta Golf Club Ⓦ www.laquintagolf.com

Museo del Bonsai (Bonsai Museum)

Some 300 bonsai specimens set in attractive Japanese-style gardens.
ⓐ Parque Arroyo de la Represa ❶ 952 86 29 26 ⏲ 10.30–13.30, 17.00–20.00 daily (summer); 10.30–13.30, 16.00–19.00 daily (winter)
❶ Admission charge

Museo del Grabado Español Contemporáneo (Museum of Contemporary Spanish Engravings)

Important collection of engravings in a former 17th-century hospital near the Arab city walls. It provides a comprehensive overview of Spanish artistic trends since the 19th century, including works by Picasso, Miró and Dalí.
ⓐ Calle Hospital Bazán ❶ 952 71 57 41 ⏲ 10.00–14.00, 18.00–21.00 Tues–Sat, closed Sun (summer); 11.00–14.00, 17.30–20.30 Tues–Sat, closed Sun (winter) ❶ Admission charge

Teatro Ciudad de Marbella (City Theatre)

A plush venue that attracts an impressive roster of international operas, concerts and dance shows, as well as plays in Spanish. Ticket prices can be very reasonable.

ⓐ Plaza Ramón Martinez ⓣ 952 90 31 59 ⓘ Famous names also perform at the grander hotels

EXCURSIONS
Mini-cruise

Travel by boat from Marbella to Puerto Banús. The journey takes approximately 30 minutes.

Fly Blue ⓐ Marbella Puerto Deportivo ⓣ 951 77 54 00 ⓛ Departures roughly every hour between 10.00 and 19.00 ⓘ Dolphin-watching trips are also available

Ojén

This picturesque mountain village lies about 10 km (6 miles) north of Marbella, high in the hills of the Sierra Blanca. Just beyond the village, in a forested game reserve, is the **Refugio de Juanar**, a charming hunting-lodge inn (ⓣ 952 88 10 00 ⓦ www.juanar.com). This makes a good starting point for walks through the hills, where you may catch sight of the rare Iberian ibex, a horned goat-like creature. If you don't feel energetic, just enjoy a good lunch. Ojén is on a bus route from Marbella. Jeep excursions, treks and mountain-bike hire are organised by **Monte Aventura**. Ask your rep, hotel or the tourist office for more information.

ⓐ Oficina de Turismo Rural, Plaza de Andalucía 1, Ojén ⓣ 952 88 15 19
ⓦ www.monteaventura.com

TAKING A BREAK

Bar Altamirano £ ❶ Characterful spot on a quiet square near the walls
at the back of the old town. Tiled wall plaques promise exotic sea fare:
bleaks, saurels, elephant fish. ⓐ Plaza de Altamirano ⓣ 952 82 49 32
ⓛ 13.00–16.00, 20.00–24.00 Thur–Tues, closed Wed

El Estrecho £ ❷ A real locals' tapas bar down a narrow alleyway.
ⓐ Calle San Lázaro 12 ⓣ 952 77 00 04 ⓛ 12.00–24.00 Mon–Sat,
closed Sun

Cafetería Marbella ££ ❸ A good bet for breakfast or coffee on Marbella's
smartest shopping street, near the shady Alameda Gardens. Plenty of
terrace space. ⓐ Avenida Ramón y Cajal ⓣ 952 86 11 44

La Taberna del Pintxo ££ ❹ Local branch of tapas chain where
waiters circulate with loaded trays and diners pay by the skewer.
ⓐ Avenida Miguel Cano 7 ⓣ 952 82 93 21 ⓦ www.latabernadelpintxo.com

AFTER DARK

Restaurants
Palms £ ❺ Beach café specialising in more interesting salads than
most, as well as excellent catch-of-the-day fish dishes. ⓐ Playa de Venus

Restaurante la Axarquía £ ❻ Good-value fish restaurant specialising
in paella and whole fish baked in salt. ⓐ Paseo Marítimo ⓣ 952 86 36 31
ⓛ Closed Wed

Mena ££ ❼ The terrace restaurants on the main square are geared
towards tourists, but this little place isn't bad value. Lovely setting in an

⬤ *The picturesque village of Ojén*

old house with tables under the orange trees. ⓐ Plaza de los Naranjos 10
ⓣ 952 77 15 97 ⓛ 11.00–23.00 Mon–Sat, closed Sun

La Pesquera ££ ❽ Highly rated seafood chain with traditional Spanish
décor and good *salmonete* (red mullet) and lobster. ⓐ Plaza de la Victoria
or Paseo Marítimo ⓣ 952 76 51 70/86 85 20 ⓦ www.lapesquera.com

Restaurante Buenaventura Plaza £££ ❾ A restaurant for a special
occasion, strung with fairy lights and situated off a pretty little square in
the old town. The inventive menu offers modern takes on traditional
Spanish dishes, like lobster with mushroom jam or duck with Málaga
wine. ⓐ Plaza de la Iglesia de la Encarnación 5 ⓣ 952 85 80 69

Santiago £££ ❿ A suave but rather expensive seafront restaurant
situated near the port. On offer is a splendid array of authentic
Andalusian dishes served in a lively and very Spanish atmosphere.
ⓐ Paseo Marítimo 5 ⓣ 952 77 00 78 ⓦ www.restaurantesantiago.com

Zoizoi £££ ⓫ Characterful restaurant in the old town, serving fresh
modern European cuisine. ⓐ Plaza de Altamirano ⓣ 952 85 88 68
ⓦ www.zoizoi.com ⓛ 19.30–late Mon–Sat, closed Sun ❶ Book in advance

Nightlife

Most of Marbella's liveliest nightlife centres on Puerto Banús (see
pages 39–41), or takes place in various hotels. Dress up, refuel your
wallet and head for the cocktail bars of the **Marbella Club** or the **Puente
Romano** or to Marbella's chichi Moroccan-themed garden club, **La Notte**
(ⓐ Camino de la Cruz ⓣ 952 77 76 25 ⓛ Closed Sun).

There are a few bars around Puerto Deportivo, but for some real
action head to **Dreamers** (ⓐ Carretera Cádiz Km 175 ⓣ 952 81 20 80), a
popular club spread over two floors that hosts visiting DJs and stays
open to 06.00 or 07.00 at weekends.

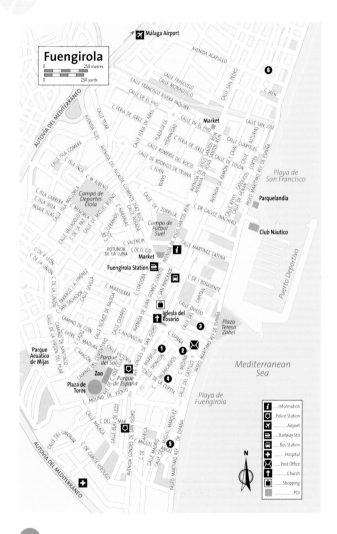

Fuengirola

Fuengirola

Fuengirola is a lively and popular seaside resort with beautiful beaches, a vibrant nightlife and lots of attractions for all ages. The beach is the centre of activity – day and night. It is lined by one of the longest promenades on the Mediterranean (it takes about two hours to walk from one end to the other). Just behind the palm-lined walkway, the old fishermen's district of Santa Fé has retained its Andalusian character. Its narrow, whitewashed streets contain some of the best restaurants in town, especially around the main square – Plaza de la Constitución – and along Calle Moncayo, nicknamed the 'Street of the Hungry'.

BEACHES

Fuengirola boasts one of the best seafronts of the entire Costa, with over 7 km (4$^1/_2$ miles) of clean, sandy beaches, divided into restaurant-beach strips, each renting out lounge chairs, parasols and pedalos. The central beaches of **Santa Amalia**, **Castillo** and **Fuengirola** lap the old town to either side of the port, while to the east the sand continues in an unending sweep past the hotel zones of **Los Boliches** and **Torreblanca**.

THINGS TO SEE & DO

Boat trips

Daily fishing trips, dolphin-spotting and sunset cruises are all on offer at the marina.

Agra Vista ☏ 952 66 66 07/679 55 40 67

Joren Maria II ☏ 952 44 48 81

Fuengirola Zoo

First-class zoo with a simulated rainforest and more than 140 animal species. ⓐ Avenida Camilo José Cela 6 ☏ 952 66 63 01 ⏱ 10.00–20.00 daily, or 24.00 in high season ⓘ Admission charge

Parque Acuático de Mijas

Children will love the water slides, rapids and surf pools at this refreshing water park, just ten minutes by bus from Fuengirola bus station. ⓐ Carretera N340, Km 209 ⓣ 952 46 04 04 ⓦ www.aquamijas.com ⓛ 10.00–19.00 daily Apr–Oct ⓘ Admission charge

Parquelandia

Swings, slides, a trampoline, a bouncy castle and mini-karting on the seafront. ⓐ Puerto Deportivo, Paseo Marítimo ⓣ 609 44 77 68 ⓛ 12.30–20.00 Mon–Fri

TAKING A BREAK

Café Fresco £ ❶ Excellent English-run restaurant with tasty organic soups, extensive salad bar, wraps, sandwiches and fresh, mixed juices like carrot, orange and ginger. ⓐ Las Rampas ⓣ 635 83 67 91

Cafetería Costa del Sol £ ❷ The place to enjoy breakfast Spanish-style – *churros* dipped into a cup of thick, sticky hot chocolate. A great cure for a hangover! ⓐ Calle Marbella 3 ⓣ 952 47 17 09

AFTER DARK

Restaurants
O Mamma Mia £ ❸ Popular, family-oriented Italian restaurant with quick, friendly service. Good value for money. ⓐ Calle de la Cruz 23 ⓣ 952 47 32 51

Monopol ££ ❹ Rustic décor, informal atmosphere and unusual, international meats, from 'Zurich veal' to 'Madagascan beef'. ⓐ Calle Palangreros 7 ⓣ 952 47 44 48 ⓛ Dinner only, closed Sun & mid-July–mid-Aug

Old Swiss House ££ ❺ *Rösti* and fondue, but plenty else too in this pleasant restaurant. ⓐ Marina Nacional 28, one block behind the beach ☎ 952 47 26 06 ⏰ 13.00–15.30, 19.00–24.00 Wed–Mon, closed Tues

La Langosta £££ ❻ Long-established restaurant specialising in lobster, as its name suggests. Mussels in saffron, sole in champagne and beef goulash are other favourites. ⓐ Lape de Vega ☎ 952 47 50 49 ⏰ 19.00–24.00 Mon–Sat, closed Sun

Nightlife

Hidden away opposite the Old Town Café and down some steps to the harbour is a long row of friendly and inexpensive bars mostly run by expats. A good bet is **The Family Bar** (☎ 952 46 16 41), a Dutch-run bar and restaurant that hosts live music every night from 20.30.

On the front line of bars overlooking the harbour, the German **Ku'Damm Berlin** (ⓐ Puerto Deportivo 12 ☎ 952 47 28 64) bar and restaurant is another popular venue that serves good food and regularly hosts live music.

Benalmádena Costa

Benalmádena Costa is a lively, purpose-built holiday resort with a wide variety of entertainment for all the family, good watersports facilities, shops, bars and restaurants appealing to all tastes and budgets. The stunning tiered marina greatly enhances the resort's appeal, and its many bars and nightclubs have made Benalmádena one of southern Spain's hottest nightspots.

Benalmádena is made up of three different districts. Cosmopolitan **Benalmádena Costa** is the main tourist centre and is focused around three main areas of entertainment – Bonanza Square, 24-Hour Square and the marina – together offering any number of things to see and do.

Further inland, tucked into the foothills of the Sierra de Mijas, **Benalmádena Pueblo** is the old part of town – the original Andalusian white village, still full of rural charm. Its sleepy, narrow streets and twisting alleyways of white-painted houses with terracotta-tiled roofs present a complete contrast to the hectic pace of the coastal strip. The main square, Plaza de España, contains the statue that has become the symbol of Benalmádena – a young girl offering water in an upturned shell.

Midway between the Pueblo and the coastline lies the main residential district, called **Arroyo de la Miel** (meaning 'Stream of Honey'). It is a busy, fashionable area with hundreds of apartment blocks and many popular restaurants, bars and clubs. Tivoli World, the resort's top children's attraction, is here, and on Fridays the local market provides a good opportunity to buy cheap provisions and local handicrafts.

BEACHES

Benalmádena boasts 9 km (5½ miles) of beaches to the west of the new marina – some sandy, some shingle, some artificial – but they are all clean and safe for swimming (**Playa Santa Ana** even has a European Blue Flag for cleanliness). **Playa Las Yucas**, between Hotel Torrequebrada and Hotel Costa Azul, is a nudist beach.

THINGS TO SEE & DO

Auditorio de Benalmádena (Benalmádena Auditorium)

Enjoy theatre, music and dance at the town's grand auditorium located next to the Parque de la Paloma. Events run throughout the year, including a festival at the end of July.

ⓐ Arroyo de la Miel ☏ 952 44 06 40

Boat trips

Take a boat to see dolphins or go on an organised mini-cruise. Some boat companies combine the trip with a visit to the Sea Life Aquarium and a mini-train ride at a special rate. Ask your holiday representative for details.

Castillo Bil-Bil

You'll spot this eye-catching crenellated Moorish building in bright reddish-pink towards the western end of the seafront. Formerly a private house, it has been converted into a gallery for temporary exhibitions. It is decorated with tiles and Arab bas-reliefs.

ⓐ Avenida Antonio Machado 78 ☏ 952 44 43 20 🕑 10.00–13.00, 15.00–20.00 daily ❶ Admission charge

⬥ *Puerto Deportivo in Benalmádena*

Golf

Benalmádena's challenging 18-hole **Torrequebrada Golf Course** (not far from town in the hills) is reputed to be a 'thinking person's course'.
ⓐ Carretera N340 ⓣ 952 44 27 41/2 ⓦ www.golftorrequebrada.com

Horse trekking

Trekking in the hills on a half-day guided excursion, ending with a barbecue back at the riding school. There's a restaurant and children's play area too.
Finca Los Caballeros ⓐ Finca Villa Vieja, Urb. Torrequebrada Norte
ⓣ 952 56 84 84 ⓦ www.fincaloscaballeros.com

Motomercado

Explore the region by bike or scooter.
ⓐ Avenida de Alay ⓣ 952 44 11 31 ⓦ www.rentabike.org

Museo de Cultura Precolombino & Arqueológico (Pre-Columbian and Archaeological Museum)

Charming little museum in the old village with an interesting collection of pre-Conquest South American artefacts and local antiquities.
ⓐ Avenida Juan Luis Peralta 49 ⓣ 952 44 85 93 ⓦ www.benalmadena.com/museo ⓛ 09.30–13.30, 18.00–20.00 Tues–Sat (summer), closed Sun & Mon; 17.00–19.00 (winter) ⓘ Admission charge

Puerto Deportivo

Looking more like a giant wedding cake than a marina, the Puerto Deportivo complex, with its countless open-air bars, restaurants and clubs, really comes to life at night. There is even underwater lighting.

Sea Life Acuario (Aquarium)

A small but excellent aquarium with walk-through water-tunnel, touch-tanks and feeding demonstrations.
ⓐ Puerto Deportivo ⓣ 952 56 01 50 ⓛ 10.00–24.00 daily
ⓘ Admission charge

> **SHOPPING**
> **Andycraft** Ethnic imports from Southeast Asia. ⓐ Dársena de
> Levante, Local 7, Puerto Deportivo ⓣ 952 57 41 53
> **La Artesanía Española** Spanish handicrafts, including ceramics,
> candles and olive wood. ⓐ 12 Avenida Antonio Machado
> **Artesanía Piel** Interesting leather goods. ⓐ Puerto Deportivo
> **La Maison en Fleur** Souvenirs and presents, including tasteful
> flower bouquets in silk and paper. ⓐ Dársena de Levante, Puerto
> Deportivo A12 ⓣ 952 56 02 99

Selwo Marina

Aquatic wildlife park housing dolphins, penguins and sea lions, as well as
a 3-D cinema and snake house.
ⓐ Parque de Paloma, Benalmádena ⓣ 952 19 04 82 ⓦ www.selwo.es
ⓒ Closed mid-Dec–mid-Feb ⓘ Admission charge

Teleférico (Cable car)

A 15-minute ride to the mountain summit, from where you can walk down.
ⓐ Arroyo de la Miel, near Tivoli ⓣ 952 57 50 38 ⓒ 10.30–01.00 daily
(summer); 10.30–21.30 daily (winter)

Tivoli World

Theme park with world-class rides, Wild West entertainment and
flamenco shows.
ⓐ Arroyo de la Miel ⓣ 952 57 70 16 ⓦ www.tivoli.es
ⓒ Eves May–Sept, until 02.00 in high season; restricted hours Sept–Apr
ⓘ No entrance fee for children under 1 m (3 ft)

TAKING A BREAK

Café Fresco £ Just like its sister-establishment in Fuengirola, this English-
run café sells excellent soups, salads, wraps and zingy fruit and veg
smoothies. ⓐ Avenida de la Constitución 17 ⓣ 618 82 68 26

Club de Buceo Los Delfines £ The popular little canteen attached to the diving school by the harbour offers unpretentious, perfectly fresh fish and good tapas. There are tables outside, and friendly service. Excellent value. ⓐ Puerto Deportivo ❶ 952 44 09 89 ⓦ www.buceolosdelfines.es ⏰ 13.00–16.30, 20.30–24.00 daily for food, 08.00–24.00 for drinks

Metro £ Inexpensive pizzas, pastas and ice creams, served indoors or on a terrace overlooking the port. Ideal for groups. ⓐ Puerto Marina ❶ 952 44 64 60 ⓦ www.metrogrupo.com

AFTER DARK

Restaurants

El Elefante £ Wholesome English home cooking accompanied by raucous entertainment seven nights a week, ranging from cabaret to hypnotists. ⓐ Benalmádena Plaza ❶ 952 56 80 57 ⓦ www.el-elefante.com ⏰ 20.30–03.00 daily

Restaurante Il Girasole £ Inexpensive restaurant serving great-quality, home-cooked fresh Italian food. ⓐ Avenida Antonio Machado ❶ 952 56 26 62

Restaurante Carretero Puerto ££ Pleasant Spanish fish restaurant with all the traditional dishes, as well as slightly more unusual ones like razor clams and seafood casserole. ⓐ Pueblo Marinero, Local E3-4 ❶ 952 56 41 90 ⏰ 13.00–17.00, 20.00–24.00 daily

Ristorante Pinocho ££ Mid-range Italian with three types of lasagne and good pizzas and ice creams, or you can cross the street to the Cafetería y Heladería Pinocho instead. ⓐ Puerto Marina ❶ 952 44 08 92 ⓦ www.pinochopuertomarina.com

Mar de Alboran £££ One of the smartest restaurants in town, near the entrance to the port, offering accomplished modern cooking with a decent wine list. A menu of the day gives you a chance to sample the

◆ *Café life in Benalmádena Pueblo*

◔ *Windmill sculpture on the Benalmádena coast road*

chef's best efforts. ⓐ Avenida de Alay 5 ⓣ 952 44 11 47 ⓦ www.marde
alboran.es ⓛ Closed Sun eve (summer); closed Sun eve & Mon (winter)

El Mero £££ Sophisticated fish restaurant with a cool terrace
over-hanging the port. Try the bream baked in salt. ⓐ Dársena de
Levante, Puerto Marina ⓣ 952 44 04 56 ⓛ 13.00–01.00 daily

Ventorillo de la Perra £££ A very typical Spanish restaurant. Both local
Malagueño cooking and general Spanish fare. ⓐ Avenida de la
Constitución 115, Arroyo de la Miel ⓣ 952 44 19 66 ⓛ 13.00–15.00,
19.30–23.30 Tues–Sun, closed Mon

Nightlife

Bar Maracas ££ Samba the night away at this buzzing nightspot. Arrive
before 24.00 as queues can be long. Be warned – dancing on the bar is a
regular occurrence. ⓐ Puerto Deportivo 107 ⓣ 952 56 64 70

Casino Torrequebrada ££ Take your passport and try your luck at the
tables. Remember to dress up. ⓐ Avenida del Sol ⓣ 952 57 73 00
ⓦ www.casinotorrequebrada.com ⓛ 21.00–05.00 daily

Joy ££ A popular club in the Marina area, attracting locals and visitors
alike. Regular live music. ⓐ Puerto Marina ⓣ 952 56 34 44
ⓛ 23.00–06.00 daily ⓘ Admission charge

Kiu ££ One of the biggest discos in town, with three DJs and three
dance floors, playing Latin, dance and chart music. ⓐ Plaza Solymar (just
off 24-Hour Square) ⓣ 952 44 05 18 ⓛ 23.00–06.30 daily (until 07.30
Fri & Sat) ⓘ Admission charge

Sala de Fiestas Fortuna £££ Hotel Torrequebrada's cabaret act is a
spectacular show. ⓐ Avenida del Sol ⓣ 952 44 60 00 ⓛ 10.30–00.30
Tues–Sat ⓘ Admission charge includes dinner and entry to the casino

⬥ *Torremolinos is a world-famous resort for sun-worshippers*

Torremolinos

The tourist boom of the 1950s, which made the Costa del Sol a world-famous holiday destination, all began in Torremolinos – a tiny fishing village turned big, brash resort. Few places in southern Spain can offer as many hotels, bars and discos, and, for sun-worshippers, 'Torrie' offers some of the best beaches on the coast.

It once had a reputation for being a downmarket resort, but recently it has shaken off this 'Terrible Torrie' image by smartening up the town and building an elegant beach promenade. By night, the neon-lit streets of the attractive old town throng with life until the early hours.

La Carihuela (the westernmost district of the resort) is a reminder of Torrie's humble beginnings as a simple fishing village. Its atmospheric, whitewashed streets are crammed with restaurants, and fishermen still barbecue silvery sardines on wooden skewers on the beach.

BEACHES

You can find some of the best beaches of the Costa here, notably the two main beaches of **Playamar** and **Bajondillo**. Then there is **Playa de la Carihuela** fringing Torrie's original fishing village to the west, and the quieter **Playa de los Alamos** to the east. All have sunbeds, umbrellas and pedalos to rent, as well as showers, café-bars and restaurants. At the height of summer, there are often beach volleyball and football competitions. Watersports are available at nearby Benalmádena marina.

THINGS TO SEE & DO

Aqualand

The largest water park in Europe, with wave machines, a 'water mountain' and 30 water slides.

ⓐ Calle Cuba 10 ⓣ 952 38 88 88 ⓦ www.aqualand.es

ⓛ 11.00–18.00 daily (May, June & Sept); 10.00–19.00 daily (July–Aug)

ⓘ Admission charge

Crocodile Park

Excellent nature park dedicated to crocs, with live demonstrations and a mini-zoo.

🅐 Calle Cuba 14 🕿 952 05 17 82 🌐 www.crocodile-park.com 🕐 10.00–19.00 daily (July–Sept); 10.00–17.00 daily (Oct–Apr) ❶ Admission charge

El Ranchito

If you are unable to get to Jerez to see the dancing horses, come here to this similar but smaller show. Horse-trekking expeditions also offered.

🅐 Senda del Pilar 4 🕿 952 38 30 63 ❶ Dressage demonstrations each Wed at 17.45 – book through your hotel

AFTER DARK

Restaurants

Restaurant Chino Sanda £ Cheap, cheerful Chinese restaurant.
🅐 Avenida Lido 6, Nuevo Playamar 🕿 952 38 09 40 🕐 12.00–16.30, 18.30–24.00 daily

Restaurante Nuevo Playamar £ Just next to 'Bar el Guíri' (the Englishman's bar) is a restaurant that is the complete opposite – very Spanish. Delicious and reasonably priced fried fish is served to a mostly local crowd. 🅐 Avenida del Lido 10 🕿 952 37 16 75 🕐 Closed Sat

La Alcena ££ Small but tasty menu of simply cooked meat and fish.
🅐 Doña María Barrabino 11 🕿 952 38 72 02 🕐 13.00–16.00, 20.00–23.00 Mon–Sat, closed Sun

Pepe y Carmen ££ Paella is the speciality at this friendly, beachside café-restaurant. 🅐 Paseo Marítimo 16 🕿 952 37 46 95

Restaurante Casa Paco la Carihuela ££ Established in 1969, this ever-popular fish restaurant is one of the best in the area. 🅐 Paseo Marítimo de la Carihuela 🕿 952 05 13 81 🕐 Closed Mon

SHOPPING

Cortefiel It's easy to pick up a bargain in this fashionable clothes store, especially during the summer sales. ⓐ Avenida Palma de Mallorca ① 952 37 02 12 ⓛ Mon–Sat

Lepanto Superb patisserie. Try the strawberry tartlets or home-made mango ice cream. ⓐ Calle San Miguel 54 ① 952 38 66 29

Frutos £££ A great place for spotting celebrities and enjoying Andalusian specialities. ⓐ Avenida de la Riviera 80 ① 952 38 14 50 ⓛ Closed Sun eve

A bewildering number of bars and restaurants line La Carihuela's long seafront. Some of the best include **Casa Guaquin** (ⓛ Closed Mon) and its neighbour **El Roqueo** (① 952 38 49 46 ⓛ Closed Tues), at Calle Carmen 35 and 37. **Casa Juan** (① 952 37 35 12) and **La Jábega** (① 952 38 63 75) are both on Calle del Mar at Nos 14 and 17.

Nightlife

Palladium £ Regularly packed solid with visitors dancing to the latest rave sounds. ⓐ Avenida Palma de Mallorca 36 ① 952 38 42 89 ⓛ 23.00–06.00 daily ① Admission charge

Eugenios ££ A long-established disco and piano bar in 'Torrole', one of the last remaining clubs in the Pueblo Blanco area. ⓐ Calle Casa Blanca 22 ① 952 38 11 31 ⓦ www.eugeniosdiscopianobar.com

El Open Arms ££ If dancing's not your thing, try karaoke until the early hours. ⓐ Plaza la Nogalerak ① 952 35 21 00 ⓦ www.elopenarms.com

Veronia ££ Music ranges from *sevillanas* to the latest chart toppers at this lively nightclub near the centre of town. ⓐ Avenida Salvador Allende 10 ① 952 37 34 70 ⓦ www.discoveronia.com ⓛ 23.00–late daily

Tarifa

Tarifa has long been popular with windsurfers and kite-surfers, but is fast becoming a major destination for beach lovers as well. The long white strand which stretches all the way from Tarifa's fortified old town to Bolonia is unsurpassed in the region, and the Atlantic water is generally very clear. But what makes Tarifa a standout destination is its laid-back bohemian vibe.

THINGS TO SEE & DO

Dolphin & whale watching

Glass-bottom boats ply the Straits on the lookout for dolphin and pilot whales, which are regularly spotted in the area. Orca, which appear in late summer in search of tuna migrating through the Straits, are a magnificent sight. Try the following:

Turmares Tarifa, which promises a 90 per cent chance of a sighting. ⓐ Avenida Alcalde Juan Nuñez 3 ⓣ 956 68 07 41 ⓦ www.turmares.com **Whale Watch España** ⓐ Avenida de la Constitución 6 ⓣ 956 68 22 47 ⓦ www.whalewatchtarifa.net

Windsurfing & kite-surfing

Tarifa is firmly established as the windsurfing capital of Europe, and is hugely popular with kite-surfers too. There are lots of kite schools offering courses for every level, many of them residential.

Tarifa Max (ⓐ Carretera Cádiz, Málaga KM 340 ⓣ 696 55 82 27 ⓦ www.tarifamax.net) and **Hot Stick Kite School** (ⓐ Calle Batalla del Salado ⓣ 956 68 04 19 ⓦ www.hotsticktarifa.com) are good places to start. The windsurfing/kite-surfing season runs from March to November, though some schools are open all year round.

TAKING A BREAK

Bossa ££ This small, English-owned, whitewashed bar is easily found, tucked away to the left of the Puerta de Jerez as you enter the old town.

It's a great spot for breakfasts, and also offers Wi-Fi Internet access and happy-hour cocktails (17.00–21.00). ❷ Puerta de Jerez ❶ 956 68 25 96 ❶ 10.00–14.00, 17.00–03.00 daily (Mar–Dec)

Café Central ££ Just a stone's throw away from the main church, this Tarifa institution is always thronging with people. The restaurant has been running since the 19th century, but the menu is more modern than most. ❷ Calle Sancho IV El Bravo 10 ❶ 956 62 70 25 ❶ 09.00–01.00 daily

100% FUN ££ This chilled-out hotel complex opposite Valdevaqueros Beach includes an excellent Tex-Mex restaurant and chilled-out bar. ❷ Carretera Cádiz–Málaga Km 76 ❶ 956 68 03 30 ❶ www.100x100fun. com ❶ Lunch and dinner, closed Nov–Feb

AFTER DARK

Mandrágora ££ Cute little Moroccan restaurant tucked away behind the church in Tarifa's old town, with expertly cooked tagines and couscous, as well as more unusual specialities like *berenjenas bereber* (aubergines stewed with spices). No reservations, so arrive early. ❷ Calle Independencia 3 ❶ 956 68 12 91 ❶ www.mandragoratarifa.com ❶ 19.30–24.00 Mon–Sat, closed mid-Dec–Mar

Taco Way & Soul Café ££ Two separate establishments which merge into one and attract a bohemian crowd for their fresh mint *mojitos* and Spanish dance music. ❷ Calle Santísima Trinidad ❶ **Taco Way** from 20.00, **Soul Café** from 21.30, closed Nov–Mar

La Vaca Loca ££ There are no starters or puddings on offer at this *churrascaria* (steakhouse): the meaty business is its raison d'être. All dishes come with potatoes and salads and the meat is absolutely delicious, especially the *secreto ibérico*. Reservations are not taken. ❷ Calle de Cervantes 6 ❶ 18.30–02.00 Mon–Sat, 12.00–02.00 Sun

Bolonia

About 15 km (9 miles) north of Tarifa, Bolonia is a minute village that comes alive in the summer, when locals flock to its pristine beach to sunbathe. In the winter, it has a desolate feel, but is still beautiful for walks into the wooded sand dunes or to explore the ruins of a Roman amphitheatre across the road. At the time of writing, there were plans to develop the ruins as a formal museum attraction.

TAKING A BREAK

Chiringuito Bar La Duna £ Simple beachfront restaurant with the freshest of fish and fantastic views from the pretty terrace all the way to Africa. Try the *choco en su tinta* (small squid in its own ink).
❸ Playa Bolonia s/n ❶ 669 45 67 07 ❺ Lunch Mar–Oct, lunch and dinner July–Aug

Chiringuito Los Troncos £ Just next door, this super-friendly beach restaurant is run along very similar lines and offers *pez espada* (swordfish) as its house speciality. ❸ Playa Bolonia s/n ❶ 956 68 86 03 ❺ 12.00–24.00 daily (mid-Mar–Nov)

◔ *The Roman remains at Bolonia*

Zahara de los Atunes

Until a few years ago, Zahara de los Atunes was the undiscovered secret of this stretch of coast, largely thanks to the fact that it is only accessed via a long curving road off the main Cádiz–Algeciras thoroughfare. These days, the village is starting to attract attention – and the inevitable new housing developments that come with it – but it still functions primarily as a centre for tuna fishing (hence the name) and retains much of its old-world charm. The beach here is white, sandy and clean, and there is no shortage of tempting restaurants, while the sleepy town itself is dominated by the ruins of the Castillo de las Amadrabas, built in the 15th century for protection against pirates and later used by fishermen to store their equipment.

⬥ *Perfect white sand at Zahara de los Atunes*

TAKING A BREAK

Pericayo ££ Tucked away up a quiet street, and hung with cured hams and dried peppers, this long-established restaurant offers a piece of old-fashioned Spain. The meat and fish are both excellent, or you could try both at once with the house speciality of *solomillo ibérico a la anchoa* (steak with anchovies). ⓐ Calle Illustre Fregona 7 ⓣ 956 43 93 15 ⓛ Lunch and dinner (Easter–Sept)

El Refugio ££ This informal restaurant specialises in home-made regional cuisine, served on a shady terrace with views to the sea. The *tortillitas de camerones casares* (shrimp fritters) and the *guisos zahareños* (stews) are especially popular. ⓐ Currita 10 ⓣ 685 86 87 14 ⓛ Lunch and dinner

Restaurant La Atarraya ££ Friendly restaurant with rustic stone walls and wooden beams on the ceilings, specialising in seafood. The *pescado a la sal* (fish baked whole in salt) is particularly good. Eat inside or under a shaded canopy overlooking the street. ⓐ Avenida de Playa s/n ⓣ 956 43 95 76 ⓛ 10.00–00.30 daily

AFTER DARK

In the summer months, the beachfront is busy with *chiringuito* restaurants that turn into lively bars at night, and the **Discoteca los Tarujos (££)** opens inside the ruined castle walls. For an evening drink in a more formal atmosphere, head to **Hotel Gran Sol (£££)**.

⬤ *The cathedral in Málaga*

EXCURSIONS
Out & about

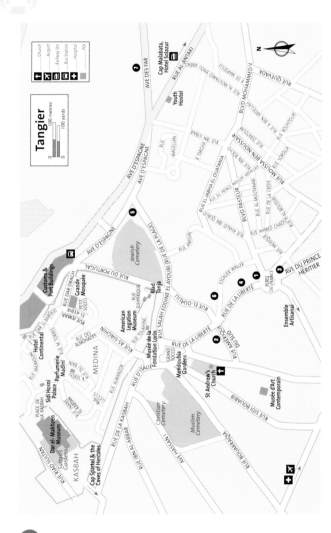

Tangier

Tangier

A city with a bohemian past and the grandeur of a bygone era, Tangier, its lustre now slightly faded, remains a fascinating place to explore. Bustling and exciting, even quite seedy in parts, it is certainly not for the faint of heart.

In Tangier's heyday in the first half of the 20th century, residents were famous for their hell-raising antics and sense of fun. The city was well known as a place of cosmopolitan charm where the expatriate good life was lived to the full.

In this jet-setting time, anything went and it was said there was nothing one could not buy in its smoky bars and disreputable souks. Artists and writers such as Beat poets Jack Kerouac and Allen Ginsberg flocked from America and Europe, drawn to the bohemian lifestyle. It was also a haven for the stylish and affluent 'Mediterranean set', where film stars casually rubbed shoulders with the criminal underworld and other unsavoury types.

Today's Tangier, a modern port with a large tourist trade, is more calm. Many of the insalubrious nightspots and seedy dens are long gone, sparkling apartment blocks and new resort hotels sprouting daily in their place. Locals good-humouredly call themselves 'Tangerines', after the fruit that has been one of their more famous exports.

As Spain is very close – only 13 km (8 miles) across the Strait of Gibraltar – it acts as the gateway to Morocco for many tourists, who take the short hop over via the ferry (just over an hour). Be particularly careful of pickpockets and hustlers at the port entrance – fake guides will often lure tourists to shops or hotels they are paid a commission to take people to.

BEACHES

If you are not located there already (most of the resort hotels are in this area), there is a mediocre town beach near Avenue des Far which continues on from the Avenue d'Espagne. Although the backdrop of

white houses and the mountains is beautiful, the closer views of the busy port area are not very inspiring. Most of the beach is fairly clean, but the western end tends to be the most crowded and consequently the dirtiest. Attach yourself to a beach bar so that you can make use of one of the safer and more private changing cabins. Camel rides and hiring windsurfing equipment are two of the diversions on offer here; another is to watch the locals in their impromptu football matches or macho acrobatic performances on the sand.

If you go via hire car or taxi to the west of the town, there are some pleasant little sandy coves you can access not too far from the city, including **Jews' Beach**, named after the Spanish Jews who arrived on it after fleeing the Inquisition.

THINGS TO SEE & DO

American Legation Museum
A palace before it became the world's first American ambassadorial residence in 1777. Now a US National Monument, it houses an art gallery.
ⓐ Rue d'Amérique ⓣ 039 93 53 17 ⓛ 10.00–13.00, 15.00–17.00 Mon–Fri, closed Sat & Sun

▲ Tangier Bay

opping and Company Booksellers
High Street
y
mbridgeshire
7 4LJ

: 01353 645005
T Rat:VAT No: 7948456G1

-07 15 12:50   Card   4a04
SISTANT

DDUCT   QTY   Amt
braltar   1   4.90

   TOTAL   4.90
   CASH
   TOTAL TENDERED   5.00
   CHANGE

Opening Hours
Monday - Saturday: 8.45am - 6pm
Sunday: 9.30am - 5pm
www.toppingbooks.co.uk

Cap Malabata, Cap Spartel and the Caves of Hercules

Tangier Bay is guarded by two promontories. To the east, Cap Malabata and its 19th-century lighthouse – which looks somewhat more like a medieval castle – guard the entrance to the Mediterranean, offering views back to Tangier and across to Algeciras in Spain. To the west, the wild and beautiful scenery of Cap Spartel marks the northwestern tip of Africa. The beaches in the bay are decent, but can become crowded between July and August. The slightly touristy **Caves of Hercules** are nearby, and provide picturesque glimpses of the Atlantic Ocean.

The best way to reach the promontories is by taxi or hire car. Try to arrange a day rate with the taxi driver before embarking.

ⓐ Next to the Mirage Hotel ⓒ 09.00–13.00, 15.00–18.00 daily
ⓘ Admission charge

Grand Socco

This large circular market area was a much livelier place in times past. Now it tends to be a hub of blue buses, taxis and myriad other traffic – automated and human. Market women sit on the central patch of grass and peddle their wares, adding considerable colour to the proceedings with their wide-brimmed hats and red-striped cloths. Regeneration work was being carried out at the time of print, so results are yet unknown.

Kasbah

A landmark in the city, with good views of the port. Once the location for the extravagant parties of film stars and millionaires, this quarter includes luxury villas, as well as a **crafts and antiquities museum** in the 17th-century former Sultanate Palace. The Andalusian gardens are a highlight.

ⓐ Northeast of the Medina, follow Rue Ben Raisouli to Place Amrah. The museum is in the Place de la Kasbah ⓣ 039 93 20 97 ⓒ 09.00–16.00 Wed–Mon, closed Tues & Fri afternoon ⓘ Admission charge

Musée de la Fondation Lorin

Explore the history of Tangier in this fascinating museum, housed in a former synagogue. Of special interest are the displays that chronicle

some of the city's more notable visitors, including Winston Churchill.
🄐 44 Rue Touahine 🕐 039 93 03 06 🕑 11.00–13.00, 15.30–19.30 Sun–Fri,
closed Sat

Parfumerie Madini

This perfumery is famed throughout North Africa for its scents, which
are sold much cheaper than brand-name perfumes. It is the place to
purchase essential oils, creams and potions – or have a special scent
made to measure in front of you.
🄐 14 Rue Sebou (in the Medina) 🕐 039 93 43 88 🕑 10.00–13.00,
16.00–21.00 Mon–Thur & Sat; 16.00–21.00 Fri & Sat

Petit Socco and the Medina

This Medina is smaller than that of most other cities, and it is a bit
rough and ready, so keep a tight hold on your belongings. Check out the
colourful **Marché des Pauvres (Paupers' Market)** for bargains and the
Ensemble Artisanal for leather goods and carpets. The central square is
the **Petit Socco**, a somewhat rundown square with old cafés and hotels,
famous for being the haunt of expats and film stars such as Errol Flynn
and Cary Grant and the painter, Henri Matisse. The charm of the place is
in its history.

Place de France

This square was once the hub of international intrigue during World
War II. The spies may be all gone, but an atmosphere of nostalgic
mystery lingers in the Café de Paris (see page 77).

St Andrew's Church

This is a beautiful and elegant little colonial English church. Famous
expats – including the eccentric correspondent of *The Times*, Walter
Harris, who lived in Morocco from the 1890s until his death in 1933 –
are buried in the graveyard.
🄐 Rue d'Angleterre 🕑 09.30–12.30, 14.30–18.00 daily

TAKING A BREAK

Café de Paris £ ❶ This French café is a legacy of the colonial occupation. ⓐ Place de France ⓛ 06.00–23.00 daily

Dean's Bar £ ❷ Built in 1837, this drinking den has played host to almost every famous traveller who has ever passed through Tangier's city streets. ⓐ 2 Rue Amérique du Sud ⓛ 09.00–23.00 daily

Mix Max £ ❸ Popular fast-food establishment with a better-than-average menu selection and clientele. ⓐ 6 Avenue du Prince Héritier ⓛ 12.00–23.00 daily

Pâtisserie La Española £ ❹ Great cakes and pastries suitable for those seeking an elegant place to rest their feet after a full day of shopping and sightseeing. ⓐ 97 Rue de la Liberté ⓛ 08.00–22.00 daily

Restaurant Africa £ ❺ A friendly welcome and simple tasty Moroccan dishes await in this Spanish town house. ⓐ 83 Rue Salah Eddine El Ayoubi ❶ 039 93 54 36 ⓛ 10.00–23.00 daily

Restaurant Populaire la Saveur de Poisson £ ❻ This unpretentious stall serves up the best fish in town. Featuring delicious sauces and spicings that combine the best of local seasonings, it's a great place for a casual bite or more filling meal. Don't miss out on the *Seffa* (sweet couscous) dessert. ⓐ 2 Escalier Waller ⓛ 11.00–22.00 Sat–Thur, closed Fri

AFTER DARK

Pasarela ❼ A mass of bars and gardens combine in this large complex that even features an outdoor swimming pool. Summer brings out a number of regular live bands of varying quality. ⓐ Avenue des Far ⓛ 20.00–03.00 Mon–Sat, closed Sun

Ronda

The old town of Ronda is one of Andalucía's most spectacular and historic towns, famous for its breathtaking scenery, its fine Arab baths and palaces and the oldest bullring in Spain. You will only appreciate its full drama as you enter the town, split in half by a gaping river gorge, **El Tajo**. The remarkable gorge is spanned by an impressive arched bridge, while tall, whitewashed houses lean from its precipitous brink.

Local legend tells that God, fed up with the constant squabbling of the people of Ronda, sent a huge bolt of lightning down to earth and split the city in two, with the women in one half and the men in the other. This arrangement was so unpopular that they built the bridge across the gorge to reunite the community.

Today, south of the gorge, **La Ciudad** (the old Moorish town) retains its Moorish plan, with many of its fine mansions and the now-Catholic church of Santa María la Mayor, once the town's main mosque. To the north lies **El Mercadillo**, the new town.

Ronda is the most famous of Andalucía's romantic *pueblos blancos*, the so-called 'white towns' built by the Moors in the 13th century to fend off the harsh rays of the sun. Its stunning location has frequently been used in Hollywood films, including *Carmen* and *For Whom the Bell Tolls*.

There are some excellent walks around Ronda. One without too much climbing is the footpath called Paseo Blas Infante, which begins behind the *parador* (state-owned hotel housed in a historic building) and leads along the brink of the gorge. An evening stroll along here gives wonderful views. Take your camera.

THINGS TO SEE & DO

Baños Arabes (Moorish Baths)

This 13th-century bathhouse is the best-preserved example in Europe, and still functions today.

ⓐ The Riverside ⓑ 952 87 38 89 ⓒ 10.00–13.30 Tues, 09.30–15.00 Wed–Sat, 10.00–14.00 Sun, closed Mon ⓘ Admission charge

🔺 *Ronda and the impressive El Tajo gorge*

La Casa del Rey Moro (Mansion of the Moorish Kings)

This 18th-century mansion overlooking the gorge was built on much older Moorish foundations. Although not open to the public, the house has an ancient underground stairway, which leads right down to the river through terraced gardens. Cut out of the rock by Christian slaves, these 365 steps guaranteed a water supply to the people of the town, even in times of siege.

ⓐ Cuesta de Santo Domingo 17 ① 952 18 72 00 ⓛ Gardens and stairway 10.00–20.00 daily (summer); 10.00–19.00 daily (winter)
❶ Admission charge

Plaza de Toros (Bullring)

The bullring, built in 1785, is one of the oldest and most beautiful in Spain. It was here that Pedro Romero, the founder of modern bullfighting, evolved today's style of fighting bulls on foot rather than on horseback. Nowadays, the bullring is only used for special fiestas, but the museum and gift shop are well worth a visit.

ⓐ Calle Virgen de la Paz 15 ① 952 87 41 32 ⓛ 10.00–20.00 daily
❶ Admission charge

El Tajo gorge

Three bridges span the gorge: the Moorish Puente de San Miguel looks over the ancient Arab baths; the Puente Viejo (Old Bridge) was built in 1616; and the not-so-new Puente Nuevo (New Bridge), built in the late 18th century, boasts unforgettable views and is the symbol of Ronda. The gorge, at its highest point, drops over 90 m (300 ft) to the River Guadalevin below, and has a rather bloody past. The architect of the Puente Nuevo fell to his death here while attempting to catch his hat. In the 18th century, injured horses from the bullring were flung over the cliffs. During the Spanish Civil War, over 500 Nationalist prisoners were thrown into the gorge by Republicans.

TAKING A BREAK

Café Alba £ A popular breakfast spot, serving delicious coffee, piping-hot chocolate and *churros* (akin to doughnuts). ⓐ Calle Espinel 44
① 952 19 09 53

Don Miguel ££ One of Ronda's most popular restaurants serving hearty Andalusian cuisine. Fabulous views. ⓐ Villanueva 4 ⓣ 952 87 77 22

Doña Pepa ££ Well-respected, family-run restaurant offering traditional local dishes like rabbit, partridge and quail in garlic. Their separate café-bar opposite serves *bocadillos* (sandwiches) and freshly squeezed orange juice. ⓐ Plaza del Socorro 10 ⓣ 952 87 47 77 ⓛ 12.00–24.00 daily

Parador de Ronda £££ The most perfectly situated hotel in town, overlooking the ravine just next to the Puente Nuevo. The food is also delicious: expect traditional Andalusian favourites like *ajo blanco* (cold garlic soup), roast kid and rabbit. For pudding, try the local speciality *yemas rondeñas* (sweet egg yolks). ⓐ Plaza España ⓣ 952 87 75 00

AFTER DARK

Restaurants & bars
Bar Las Castañuelas £ A lively local bar where you can enjoy a glass of *fino* (sherry) accompanied by inexpensive, traditional tapas.
ⓐ Avenida Doctor Fleming 3 ⓣ 952 87 61 78

Peña Flamenco Tobalo ££ Some claim that Ronda (and not Sevilla) is the birthplace of flamenco. Live shows take place in Bar la Plazuela most Fridays. Telephone to check. ⓐ Calle de la Toma 6 ⓣ 952 87 41 77 ❶ Admission charge

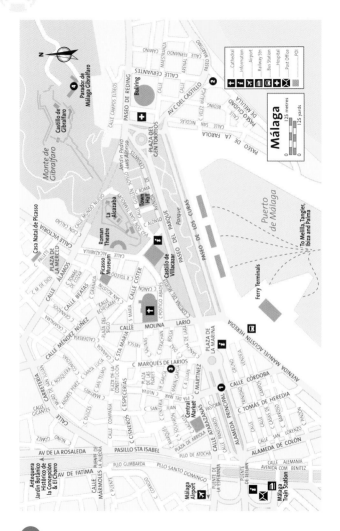

Málaga

Málaga is a bustling seaport, the sprawling capital of the Costa del Sol, the second city of Andalucía and the sixth-biggest city in Spain. You either love it or you hate it, but there is no denying, it is one of the most Spanish of cities – atmospheric and vibrant.

THINGS TO SEE & DO

La Alcazaba (Moorish Fortress)

The remains of an 11th-century Moorish fortress stand in attractive fountain-splashed gardens high above the city. Its terraces afford photogenic vistas of Málaga and its glittering bay.

ⓐ Calle Alcazabilla ⓣ 952 22 00 43 ⓛ 09.30–13.30, 17.00–20.00 Tues–Fri, 10.00–14.00 Sat & Sun, closed Mon ⓘ Admission charge

Antequera

The town of Antequera is easily reached by car or public transport from Málaga. It's usually a quiet town, but it livens up on Fridays when its market is in full swing. Most of its monuments are shut on Mondays. The old centre contains an impressive list of monuments, including several large churches, a ruined Arab fortress (Alcazaba) and an archway (Arco de los Gigantes) dating from the 16th century. Both the town hall (Palacio Consistorial) and the museum (Museo Municipal) occupy fine palaces. Antequera's most unusual sights, though, are its dolmen caves, easily found on the approach road from Málaga. These megalithic monuments are believed to be around 4,500 years old.

Castillo de Gibralfaro (Gibralfaro Castle)

One of Málaga's great landmarks, this Moorish castle perched high above the city was built sometime in the early 14th century on the site of an ancient lighthouse. At the foot of the Castillo is a Roman amphitheatre.

ⓐ Monte de Gibralfaro ⓣ 952 22 72 30 ⓛ 09.30–20.00 daily
ⓘ Joint ticket with La Alcazaba

Cathedral

Málaga's cathedral took more than 350 years to build. The original plans included two towers but the money ran out, so only one was completed, giving rise to the affectionate nickname, La Manquita ('the little one-armed woman').

ⓐ Calle Molina Lario ⓣ 952 21 59 17 ⓛ 10.00–12.45, 16.00–17.30 Mon–Sat, closed to sightseers on Sun ⓘ Admission charge

El Chorro

North of Málaga, the River Guadalhorce cuts a dramatic gorge through sheer 30-m (100-ft) cliffs that make irresistible targets for rock climbers. Above the gorge are the reservoir lakes, which supply most of Málaga's water. The scenery in this craggy area is spectacular, and offers many opportunities for walks and picnics.

Jardín Botánico Histórico de la Concepción

An Englishwoman married to the Marquis of Casa Jorge Loring began assembling this collection of rare and exotic plants in 1850. It is now one of Spain's most important gardens.

ⓐ Carretera del Jardín Botánico ⓣ 952 25 21 48 ⓛ 09.30–19.30 Tues–Sun, closed Mon ⓘ Admission charge

Picasso museums

The artist Pablo Picasso was born in Málaga in 1881. His birthplace, the **Casa Natal de Picasso**, contains an exhibition of photographs of Picasso as a child, plus memorabilia and early works.

ⓐ Plaza de la Merced ⓣ 952 06 02 15 ⓦ www.fundacionpicasso.malaga. eu.com ⓛ 09.30–20.00 daily

   In a nearby street, part of the former Museo de Bellas Artes, a 16th-century palace, has been restored to house the excellent **Picasso Museum**, containing around 140 major works. ⓐ Calle San Agustín 8 ⓣ 952 12 76 00 ⓦ www.museopicassomalaga.org ⓛ 10.00–20.00 Tues–Thur & Sun, 10.00–21.00 Fri–Sat, closed Mon ⓘ Admission charge

⬥ Shaded from the blistering sun, the main shopping street in Málaga

El Torcal

South of Antequera lies a weird wonderland of eroded limestone outcrops. This spectacular natural park is colonised by rare plants and birds of prey. The strange formations are best seen towards sundown, when the shadows are sharpest. For more information, contact the park information centre: **Centro de Visitantes £** 952 03 13 89 10.00–14.00, 15.00–17.00 daily (Nov–May); 10.00–14.00, 16.00–18.00 daily (June–Oct)

TAKING A BREAK

Málaga is famed for its old *bodegas* (wine bars) and tapas bars, which provide a good opportunity to try local delicacies and the sweet local wine, while the smart seafront promenade boasts some of the best fish restaurants in the province.

Antigua Casa del Guardia £ ❶ Atmospheric *bodega* founded in 1840, and lined with barrels. An excellent place to sample some of Málaga's sweet wines. ⓐ Alameda Principal 18 952 21 46 80

Antonio Martín £££ ❷ A popular seafront restaurant specialising in seafood. ⓐ Paseo Marítimo 952 22 73 82

AFTER DARK

Restaurants
Mesón lo Güeno ££ ❸ Elegant Spanish tapas restaurant. ⓐ Calle Marín García 9 952 22 30 48 Daily for lunch and dinner

Parador de Málaga Gibralfaro ££ ❹ This very special state-owned hotel and restaurant is set high on a wooded hill, and has breathtaking views along the coast. The food is very good, and the set menu is punctuated by tasty *amuses bouches*. ⓐ Castillo del Gibralfaro 952 22 19 02

❿ *You'll need to refresh yourself after the climb up to the Rock*

 LIFESTYLE
Gibraltar life

Food & drink

From traditional English fish and chips and pub lunches in Gibraltar, to the sophisticated restaurants of Marbella or the simple *chiringuito* bars of the Costa de la Luz, the cuisine of the Rock and its surrounding area is as wide in variety as it is rich in flavours. For centuries, Andalucía has been a land of different cultures, and their influences are reflected in the local food – the Phoenician style of salting, the Roman appreciation of olive oils and garlic, and the Arab taste for sweet dishes and exotic fruits and vegetables. The local cuisine is an ensemble of spicy dishes and bold, sun-drenched Mediterranean flavours unique to southern Spain.

Eating is also a major pastime in and around Gibraltar. Locals tend to eat late, with wine-fuelled lunches lasting from 13.00 until 17.00 and evening meals kicking off after 20.30. They will often be relatively formal affairs with plenty of courses, but more relaxed meals where everyone shares lots of smaller dishes – *tapas* or *raciones* – are also very popular.

STARTERS

One of the region's best-loved starters is chilled soup: *gazpacho andaluz* (made with tomato, garlic, sweet peppers and cucumber) is the most common but also worth a try are the thicker *salmorejo* (served with bits of egg and cured ham) and *ajo blanco* (made from garlic and almonds and served with grapes). In the winter, warm and hearty *potajes* are popular – thick vegetable soups which will often contain chunks of meat.

Other favourite starters include thinly sliced dark-cured *jamón serrano* and triangles of typical Spanish *Manchego* cheese, or mini sandwiches known as *montaditos*. Gibraltar's two home-grown specialities are also worth sharing: delicious *torta de acelga*, a pie made with red chard and whole boiled eggs, and *calentita*, a flat pie of sorts made entirely from chickpea flour and best served with plenty of salt.

MAIN DISHES

Fish: Fresh fish is one of Andalucia's staples. If you are visiting in the summer, don't miss out on barbecued sardines, which are often cooked on an open fire on the beach and usually served with lots of salt and lemon. The daily catch in most coastal towns also includes *bonito* or *atun* (tuna), *rape* (monkfish), *salmonete* (red mullet), *pez espada* (swordfish) and *lenguado* (sole) – which are all delicious pan fried or grilled (*a la plancha*). Also worth trying are *gambas al pil-pil* (prawns

🔺 *Alfresco eating in Grand Casemates Square*

⬟ Grand Casemates Square is well supplied with cafés and bars

sizzling in oil, garlic and chilli), *calamares en su tinta* (squid cooked in its own ink) and of course *paella* – a scrumptious rice dish of meat, tomatoes, peppers, onions and a heap of seafood. But for those keen to embrace Gibraltar's British roots, the novelty of traditional battered cod and mushy peas on a blazing hot summer's day is hard to beat.

Meat: In inland Spain, a rich, traditional cuisine incorporates the game and wild herbs of the mountains, with hearty meat dishes including *estofado* (meat stew), *fabada* (ham and bean stew), *conejo* (rabbit casserole) and *choto al ajo* (roast kid in garlic sauce). Look out also for *albondigas* (spicy meatballs), *calderetas* (lamb stew with almonds), and one of the most famous Andalusian dishes of all, *raba de toro* (tender oxtail prepared with tomatoes, onions and spices). Food buffs should also sample the many tasty local varieties of sausage and cured ham. *Pata negra* is the most highly prized.

DESSERTS AND SWEETS
Remember to save room for pudding – sweet, gelatinous *tocino de ciel* (flan), sticky *natillas* (cream custards), *yemas del tajo* (sweets based on egg yolks and sugar), *brazos de gitano* (cream-filled pastries) and *piononos* (liqueur-soaked cake). If all that sounds too much, lemon sorbet with cava is a refreshing way to round off a meal, or enjoy delicious fresh fruits like melon, oranges, peaches, grapes and figs.

VEGETARIAN FOOD
Vegetarians will eat well in Gibraltar, where a full range of international cuisine is served. In Andalucía, most menus are geared to meat and fish eaters but usually include a range of salads and vegetable dishes as well. Good bets include *garbanzos con espinacas* (chickpeas with spinach), *judías verdes con salsa de tomate* (green beans with tomato sauce), *pisto de verduras* (ratatouille) and the ubiquitous but delicious *tortilla* (thick omelette with potatoes). The options in Morocco are also pretty decent, with vegetable tagine, *Loubia* (white bean stew) and couscous top of the veggie list.

Menu decoder

Aceitunas aliñadas Marinated olives

A la plancha Grilled

Albóndigas de pescado Fish cakes

Albóndigas en salsa Meatballs in (usually tomato) sauce

Alioli Garlic-flavoured mayonnaise served as an accompaniment

Bistec or biftek Beef steak; rare is *poco hecho*, medium is *regular* and well done is *muy hecho* (ask for it more well cooked than at home)

Bocadillo The Spanish sandwich, usually made of French-style bread

Caldereta A stew based on fish or lamb

Caldo A soup or broth

Calentita Flat pie made of chickpea flour and best served with lots of salt, a favourite of Gibraltar

Carne Meat; *carne de ternera* is beef; *carne picada* is minced meat; *carne de cerdo* is pork; *carne de cordero* is lamb

Carne/pollo empanada Breaded meat or chicken escalope, either served hot with salad and chips, or cold in a sandwich

Chorizo A cured, dry, red-coloured sausage made from chopped pork, paprika, spices, herbs and garlic

Churros Flour fritters cooked in spiral shapes in very hot fat, best dunked into hot chocolate

Cordero asado Roast lamb flavoured with lemon and white wine

Couscous Ground semolina grains – the dietary staple of Moroccans – traditionally served with a thick meat or vegetable stew

Embutidos charcutería Pork meat preparations including *jamón* (ham), *chorizo* (see left), *salchichones* (sausages) and *morcillas* (black pudding)

Ensalada Salad; the normal restaurant salad is composed of iceberg lettuce, onion and tomato

Ensalada mixta As above, but with extra ingredients, such as boiled egg, tuna fish or asparagus

Escabeche A sauce of fish, meat or vegetables cooked in wine and served cold

Estofado de buey Beef stew made with carrots and turnips, or with potatoes

Fiambre Any type of cold meat such as ham, *chorizo*, etc

Flan Caramel custard, the national dessert of Spain

Fritura A fry-up, as in *fritura de pescado* – different kinds of fried fish

Gambas Prawns; *gambas a la plancha* are grilled and *gambas al pil-pil* are fried with garlic and chilli

Gazpacho andaluz Cold soup (originally from Andalucía) made from tomatoes, cucumbers, peppers, garlic and olive oil

Gazpacho manchego (Not to be confused with *gazpacho andaluz*.) A hot dish made with meat (chicken or rabbit) and unleavened bread

Habas con jamón Broad beans fried with diced ham

Helado Ice cream

Jamón Ham; *jamón serrano* and *jamón ibérico* (far more expensive) are dry cured; cooked ham is *jamón de york*

Langostinos Large prawns

Lenguado Sole

Mariscos Shellfish

Menestra A dish of mixed vegetables cooked separately and combined before serving

Menú del día Set menu for the day at a fixed price; it may include bread, wine and a dessert, but it doesn't usually include coffee

Paella Famous rice dish originally from Valencia but now made all over Spain; *paella valenciana* has chicken and rabbit; *paella de mariscos* is made with seafood; *paella mixta* combines meat and seafood

Pan Bread; *pan de molde* is sliced white bread; wholemeal is *pan integral*

Pincho moruno Spicy chunks of pork on a skewer

Pisto The Spanish version of ratatouille, made with tomato, peppers, onions, garlic, courgettes and aubergines

Salpicón de mariscos Seafood salad

Sopa de ajo Warming winter garlic soup thickened with bread, usually with a poached egg floating in it

Tajine Hearty Moroccan stew usually made with lamb, chicken or vegetables, and cooked very slowly in an earthenware pot

Tarta helada A popular ice-cream cake served as dessert

Torta de acelga Typical Gibraltarian pie filled with red chard and whole boiled eggs

Tortilla de patatas The classic thick omelette made with potatoes and eaten hot or cold; if you want a plain omelette ask for a *tortilla francesa*

Zarzuela de pescado y mariscos A stew made with white fish and shellfish in a tomato, wine and saffron stock

Shopping

Shopping is a priority for many visitors to Gibraltar, keen to take advantage of VAT-free perfume, cosmetics, alcohol and cigarettes. There is also a wide range of items to buy and places to buy them in the surrounding area in Spain, ranging from seaside fleamarkets to upmarket fashion boutiques. In Gibraltar, shops tend to follow British opening hours, 09.00–17.30, rather than Spanish opening hours which include a lunchtime siesta and open late into the evening.

● *Head for Gibraltar's Main Street for VAT-free shopping*

GIFTS & HANDICRAFTS

The best holiday buys here are local handicrafts, including lace, colourful ceramics and attractive basketwork. You will find plenty of choice in the craft shops of Ronda and other mountain villages. Good buys include leather goods, embroidered shawls and ceramics.

FASHIONS

Marbella and central Málaga are probably the best places for clothes shopping, with their chic boutiques and fashion stores. For trendy designer boutiques and a glamorous backdrop of millionaires' yachts, Puerto Banús is a shopper's paradise, even just for window-shopping. More affordable are Torremolinos' Calle San Miguel and Gibraltar's Main Street, where you can find everything from jewellery and cosmetics to leather goods and Lladro porcelain at VAT-free prices. There is a good range of electronics stores and familiar UK fashion chains such as Marks & Spencer, Topshop, Monsoon and BHS, but these don't offer the same VAT-free bargains. The Costa del Sol is also a good place to buy sports clothing and equipment, especially at the end of the season.

MARKETS

Bargain hunters will love the hustle and bustle of the local markets. The best buys are fruit and vegetables, leather goods, ceramics and lace. Don't forget to barter; this is very normal at markets in Spain and Morocco, so you won't be offending anyone – it's also great fun. Most major resorts along the coast have a morning market once a week. Gibraltar has a lively daily indoor food market close to Grand Casemates Square, but Fuengirola Market (Tues) has the reputation of being the biggest, cheapest and best. If you are in Gibraltar on a Wednesday, cross the border to La Línea's *Miércoles Loco* (literally Crazy Wednesday) where bargain-hunting locals buy everything from clothes and jewellery to pottery and bed linen at knock-down prices.

Children

There is plenty to amuse children in Gibraltar and the surrounding area. Apart from the obvious pleasures of the beach or the hotel pool, the region has masses of attractions aimed at youngsters of all ages. Many of the hotels organise children's programmes of fun, games and outings, and tourist offices have comprehensive lists of all the local attractions geared towards children.

ANIMAL MAGIC
There is a whole host of animal-orientated activities along the coast which are fun for children – with the Apes' Den in Gibraltar at the top of the list (see pages 17–18). The monkeys are bold enough to sit on your shoulder, but do not feed them as they are wild and can give a nasty nip. Other wildlife attractions in the region include the Fuengirola Zoo (see page 51), the Crocodile Park and the spectacular shows of Andalusian horse dressage at El Ranchito, both near Torremolinos (see page 64).

BOAT TRIPS
Older children will relish the idea of a boat excursion to explore the coastline. Most resorts offer trips, and many include opportunities for swimming, diving and snorkelling. Gibraltar also has particularly good dolphin-spotting trips, often in glass-bottom boats.

FAMILY RESTAURANTS
Gibraltarians and Spaniards adore children, which means they are welcome in restaurants, even late at night. Some have high chairs available and most have children's choices on the menu.

MINI-TRAINS AND CABLE CARS
Most resorts have a mini-train, enabling parents to see the sights while keeping the children happy. Gibraltar also has a popular cable car which is a less arduous way of getting to the top of the Rock, and offers splendid views.

SPORTS

When the family has tired of the beach, why not have a quick round of mini-golf, take them horse riding or try a few circuits of go-karting? Older children may also be interested in kite-surfing and windsurfing, with two-day starter courses offered in windy Tarifa.

THEME PARKS AND FAIRS

There are lots of thrills to be had in Tivoli World, the largest amusement park on the Costa del Sol (see page 57). Children can have a go on their favourite rides like the waltzers, the big wheel, the genuinely scary ghost train and the dodgems, as well as seeing some traditional flamenco, Western or circus shows. Most resorts also have an evening fair during the summer, with all the usual rides. Local children dress up in flamenco outfits.

WATER FUN PARKS

A splashing time is guaranteed for all at Aqualand in Torremolinos (see page 63) and the Parque Acuático de Mijas, just outside Fuengirola (see page 52), with a wide variety of activities including the largest water slide in Europe, wave machines, rapids and a park for small children.

⬤ *Gibraltar's cable car is very popular*

Sports & activities

CYCLING

Cycling and mountain biking are excellent ways to enjoy the Andalusian countryside. The tourist board has a guide covering 120 itineraries, with maps, hill profiles, time required and difficulty ratings available from most tourist information offices. Two reliable bike-hire shops are **Motomercado** ⓐ Avenida Jesús Santos Rein 47, Los Boliches, Fuengirola ⓣ 952 47 25 51 ⓦ www.rentabike.org; and **Xtrem Bike** ⓐ Las Mercedes 14, Torremolinos ⓣ 952 38 06 91

GOLF

The Costa del Sol is often called the Costa del Golf, and not without reason. With 40-plus courses within just 120 km (75 miles) of coastline, it is Europe's number one winter golf destination, with some of the finest courses in the world. Most courses demand a handicap certificate, and in high season (Jan–May & Sept–Nov) book tee-times well in advance.

Los Arqueros Golf Founded by world champion Manuel Pinero – tuition at all levels. ⓐ Carretera de Ronda, Km 42.9 ⓣ 952 78 46 00

La Dama de Noche A nine-hole course, offers floodlit golf, enabling tee off as late as 22.00. ⓐ Camino del Ángel, Marbella ⓣ 952 81 81 50

Marbella Golf and Country Club ⓐ Carretera N340, Km 187 ⓣ 952 83 05 00

Mijas Golf ⓐ Carretera Coín, Km 3 ⓣ 952 47 68 43

Sotogrande ⓐ Carretera N340, Km 130 ⓣ 956 78 50 14

Valderrama Setting of the 1997 Ryder Cup. ⓐ Carretera N340, Km 132 ⓣ 956 79 12 00

HORSE RIDING

Centro Hípico Hoppla near Fuengirola offers horse rental and excursions. ⓐ Calle Enterrios 49, Mijas Costa ⓣ 952 11 90 74

Lakeview Equestrian Centre in San Pedro organises lessons for adults and children, as well as treks in the countryside. ⓐ Urbanización Valle del Sol, San Pedro ⓣ 952 78 69 34

JEEP SAFARIS

Discover rural Spain by jeep with **Marbella Rangers** (📞 952 83 30 82) or **Niza Cars** of Torremolinos (📞 952 38 14 48).

SCUBA DIVING

The sheltered Bay of Gibraltar is a good place for beginners, and also has the added attractions of an artificial reef rich in sea life and a whole host of sunken shipwrecks to explore. Useful contacts include: **Dive Charters** in Gibraltar's Marina Bay 📞 200 45649

SKIING

Northeast of Málaga, the Sierra Nevada is the most southerly ski region in Europe and one of the highest. Its most popular ski resort is just 31 km (19 miles) from the city of Granada: **Solynieve** 📞 958 24 91 00 🌐 www.skireport.com/spain for ski reports

WATERSKIING

Waterskiing is available from most marinas and also at **Funny Beach**, the watersports centre just east of Marbella (📍 Carretera N340, Km 184 📞 952 82 33 59 🌐 www.funnybeach.net). Alternatively, **Cable Ski Marbella** offers the perfect way for beginners to learn – in calm waters and without a boat! Instead, an overhead cable takes you round an 800-m (1/2-mile) circuit (📍 Guadalmina Alta, Parque de las Medranas s/n, 29670 San Pedro de Alcàntara 📞 952 78 55 79 🌐 www.cableski marbella.es).

WINDSURFING & KITE-SURFING

Tarifa has long been known as the windsurfing capital of Europe, but it has more recently established itself as the Continent's top destination for kite-surfing as well. In good wind conditions in the summer, it isn't unusual to count more than 300 kites over the sea. **Tarifa Max** (📞 696 55 82 27 🌐 www.tarifamax.net) and **Hot Stick Kite School** (📞 956 68 04 19 🌐 www.hotsticktarifa.com) are good places to start. The main windsurfing/kite-surfing season runs from March to November.

Festivals & events

FESTIVALS

Every town in Spain has a *feria* (festival) to celebrate its patron saint's day, and these festivals usually involve lively parades, music, dancing, food, wine, street processions and sometimes bullfights, funfairs and circuses. At night, vast paellas are cooked over an open fire and the celebrations continue with singing, flamenco and fireworks. The largest and most spectacular is in Málaga in August. For more details, consult Ⓦ www.andalucia.com/festival

Gibraltar hosts a small *feria* in late August, and joins in with the one just across the border in La Línea for the last two weeks of July.

The other big events on the Rock include:

Calentita! (early June) Annual food festival celebrating the different cuisines of the Rock's many ethnic groups and named after one of Gibraltar's official national dishes. Most activity takes place in Grand Casemates Square.

Miss Gibraltar (end of June) Gibraltar hosts an amazing amount of beauty pageants and while many residents approach with tongue firmly in cheek, everyone takes notice of the annual Miss Gibraltar contest. The 2009 winner, Kaiane Aldorino, went on to win Miss World.

National Day (10 September) Everybody wears red and white and takes to the streets for a day of singing, performances, speeches and widespread boozing on this politically motivated annual holiday. The day culminates in a spectacular firework display at the harbour.

Three Kings Festival (5 January) Catholic Gibraltar follows the Spanish tradition of celebrating the Epiphany, when the three kings arrived in Bethlehem to see the newborn baby Jesus. Crowds turn out for an annual street parade complete with real-life camels.

⬥ *The mesmerising excitement of a flamenco display*

○ Colourful boats adorn the beaches

VIRGEN DEL CARMEN

If you happen to take a holiday on the Costa del Sol on 16 July, you should make an effort to catch this colourful and lively fiesta. Essentially, it's a 'blessing of the waters' ceremony, a reminder that those big holiday resorts were once just simple fishing communities. There are several days of events, which culminate in a splendid procession in which the patron saint of fishermen is carried from the church into the sea. The celebrations take place in several locations, but are especially magnificent in **Los Boliches, Fuengirola**.

❿ *It may seem strange to see British bobbies in the Mediterranean*

 PRACTICAL INFORMATION
Tips and advice

Accommodation

The following is a brief selection of hotels in the area, graded by approximate price:

£ budget   ££ mid-range   £££ expensive

BOLONIA

Hostal Bellavista £ Low-key, family-run hotel with great sea views.
ⓐ Bellavista 21, Bolonia ⓣ 956 68 85 53

ESTEPONA

Hotel Mediterráneo £ Simple one-star hotel facing the sea and a short walk from Estepona's old town centre. Recommended budget option.
ⓐ Avenida de España 68, Estepona ⓣ 952 79 33 93

FUENGIROLA

Hostal Marbella £ Quaint little family-run hotel in one of the nicest streets in Fuengirola town centre, and a short walk from the beach.
ⓐ Calle Marbella 34, Fuengirola ⓣ 952 66 45 03
ⓦ www.hostalmarbellainfo.com

GIBRALTAR

Cannon Hotel £ Centrally located just off Main Street, this friendly hotel is Gibraltar's best budget option. It is well suited to families, with one-, two- and three-person rooms and a choice of en-suite or shared bathrooms. ⓐ 9 Cannon Lane, Gibraltar ⓣ 200 51711
ⓦ www.cannonhotel.gi

Bristol Hotel ££ The entrance to the Bristol is smarter and more spacious than some of its rooms, but they're still not bad value given the hotel's very central location, just off Gibraltar's Main Street. Facilities include a small swimming pool. ⓐ 8/10 Cathedral Square, Gibraltar ⓣ 200 76800
ⓦ www.bristolhotel.gi

Queen's Hotel ££ This old-fashioned hotel also styles itself as Gibraltar's best budget option. It has a friendly, family-run atmosphere and its location just outside the city walls means it is well placed for both the town centre and the Upper Rock. ⓐ 1 Boyd Street, Gibraltar ⓣ 200 74000 or 200 41682 ⓦ www.queenshotel.gi

The Caleta Hotel £££ Perched on the eastern face of the Rock itself, the Caleta commands fantastic views across the water to Spain and down to the charming Catalan Bay beach below. It is a bit more of a schlep to town than some of the other options, but well worth it. The modern décor is pleasant and the food is good. ⓐ Sir Herbert Miles Road, Gibraltar ⓣ 200 76501 ⓦ www.caletahotel.com

The Rock Hotel £££ A Gibraltarian institution with unsurpassed views to Africa, which make up for the ten-minute walk from town. The hotel itself dates back to the 1930s and is still possessed of an old-fashioned feel, as well as a casino and a swimming pool. ⓐ 3 Europa Road, Gibraltar ⓣ 200 73000 ⓦ www.rockhotelgibraltar.com

MÁLAGA

Hotel NH Málaga ££ This very comfortable modern hotel is well placed for making the most of Málaga's shopping and sightseeing opportunities. It comes equipped with all the usual facilities, including a gym, two bars and a restaurant. ⓐ Avenida Río Guadalmedina, Málaga ⓣ 952 07 13 23 ⓦ www.nh-hotels.com

PUERTO BANÚS

Hotel H10 Andalucía Plaza £££ Plush four-star hotel with swimming pool, Turkish baths, casino and two different restaurants in one of the most upmarket districts on the Costa del Sol. ⓐ Urbanización Nueva Andalucía, Puerto Banús ⓣ 952 24 32 42 ⓦ www.h10hotels.com

RONDA

Hotel Royal £ Cheap and cheerful *pensión* (small, family-run hotel) 150 m (164 yds) from Ronda's bullring, with clean rooms and friendly staff. ⓐ Virgen de la Paz 42, Ronda ⓣ 952 87 11 41

TARIFA

100% FUN ££ Just across the road from the beautiful Valdevaqueros beach, 100% FUN is a good bet for families, with well-priced chalets set about tended gardens. Facilities include a swimming pool, an excellent Tex-Mex restaurant and chilled-out bar, and the hotel is happy to organise kite-surfing, boogie-board hire and other activities. ⓐ Carretera Cádiz–Málaga Km 76, Tarifa ⓣ 956 68 03 30 ⓦ www.100x100fun.com ⓛ Closed Nov–Feb

TORREMOLINOS

Hotel Los Jazmines ££ Towerblock hotel with its own swimming pool and gardens, a good walk from Torremolinos town but just across the road from the beach and a number of good *chiringuitos* (beach restaurants/bars). ⓐ Avenida del Lido 6, Torremolinos ⓣ 952 38 50 33 ⓦ www.hotellosjazmines.com

ZAHARA DE LOS ATUNES

Hotel Doña Lola Zahara ££ Excellent-value three-star hotel with helpful staff and something of a luxury feel. ⓐ Plaza Thomson 1, Zahara de los Atunes ⓣ 956 43 90 09 or 956 43 90 68 ⓦ www.donalazahara.com

Preparing to go

GETTING THERE

Gibraltar and the surrounding areas are easily reached by plane, with regular flights direct to Gibraltar, Málaga, Sevilla, Jerez and Tangier on British Airways and the Spanish national airline Iberia as well as budget carriers. The low-cost airline Monarch flies from London Luton and other non-London airports around the UK to Gibraltar, Málaga and Jerez. Ryanair covers the routes from London Stansted and Ireland to Málaga, Sevilla and Jerez, while easyJet serves Gibraltar and Málaga from London Gatwick. The number of direct flights to Gibraltar is likely to increase. The websites Ⓦ www.opodo.co.uk and Ⓦ www.expedia.co.uk are useful for tracking down the cheapest deals.

In July and August, when prices tend to rise considerably, package holidays may offer the best value. If your travelling times are flexible, and you can avoid the school holidays, look for cheap last-minute deals on websites such as Ⓦ www.lastminute.com or in papers like *The Sunday Telegraph*, *The Sunday Times* and *The Mail on Sunday*.

Alternatively, you can travel by ferry, which may work out cheaper for families taking their own car. At the time of writing, there are six crossings from the UK to Spain each week, including a 29-hour trip from Portsmouth to Bilbao with P&O or a 19-hour crossing from Plymouth to Santander with Brittany Ferries. Try Ⓦ www.directferries.co.uk. Another idea if you want to combine a break on the coast with some sightseeing in the Spanish interior is to cross to France by ferry or Eurostar, and travel all the way to Gibraltar by train or car. It is best to go via Madrid and allow three to four days with a few stops.

British Airways ❶ 0844 493 0707 Ⓦ www.britishairways.com
easyJet ❶ 0871 244 2366 (premium rate number) Ⓦ www.easyjet.com
Iberia ❶ 0870 609 0500 Ⓦ www.iberia.com
Monarch ❶ 08700 405 040 Ⓦ www.monarch.co.uk
Ryanair ❶ 08712 460 000 (Great Britain) or 0818 303 030 (Ireland)
Ⓦ www.ryanair.com

INSURANCE

Have you got sufficient cover for your holiday? Check that your policy covers you adequately for loss of possessions and valuables, for activities you might want to try – such as scuba diving, horse riding or watersports – and for emergency medical and dental treatment, including flights home if required.

The EHIC card replaced the old E111 form and entitles British citizens to reduced-cost and sometimes free state-provided medical treatment in the EEA. For further information, ring the EHIC enquiries line ☎ 0845 605 0707 or visit ⓦ www.ehic.org.uk

Many people are aware that air travel emits CO_2, which contributes to climate change. You may be interested in the possibility of lessening the environmental impact of your flight through the charity Climate Care, which offsets your CO_2 by funding environmental projects around the world. Visit ⓦ www.jpmorganclimatecare.com

Brittany Ferries ☎ 08709 076 103 ⓦ www.brittany-ferries.co.uk
Interrail ☎ 08700 841 410 ⓦ www.interrailnet.com
P&O Ferries ☎ 08705 980 333 ⓦ www.poferries.com

TOURISM AUTHORITY

For information about Gibraltar, contact the **Gibraltar Information Bureau** ➌ Arundel Great Court, 179 The Strand, London WC2R 1EH ☎ 020 7836 0777 ⓦ www.gibraltar.gov.uk

The **Spanish National Tourist Office** is at ➋ 22–23 Manchester Square, London W1M 5AP ☎ 020 7486 8077. It is best to write or visit in person, or you can consult the Spanish National Tourist Office website at ⓦ www.tourspain.co.uk

The **Moroccan National Tourist Board** is at ➌ 205 Regent Street, London W1B 4HB ☎ 020 7437 0073 ⓦ www.tourism-in-morocco.com

Another useful site dedicated to living and holidaying in southern Spain is W www.andalucia.com, while W www.visitcostadelsol.com deals specifically with the Costa del Sol.

BEFORE YOU LEAVE

It is not necessary to have inoculations to travel in Europe, but make sure you and your family are up to date with the basics, such as tetanus. If you plan to make an excursion to Morocco, it is mandatory to have your tetanus and polio immunisations up to date.

It is also a good idea to pack a well-stocked first-aid kit. Sun lotion can be more expensive than in the UK so it is worth taking a good selection. Take enough of your prescription medicines with you – they may be difficult to obtain in Spain and Morocco. It is also worth having a dental check-up before you travel.

ENTRY FORMALITIES

The most important documents you will need are your tickets and your passport. Check well in advance that your passport is up to date and has at least three months left to run. All children, including newborn babies, need their own passport. It generally takes at least three weeks to process a passport renewal. For the latest information, contact the **Passport Agency** ☎ 0870 521 0410 W www.ukpa.gov.uk

For Spain: Citizens of the UK, Ireland, other EU countries, the USA, Canada, Australia and New Zealand do not require a visa for stays of up to 90 days. South Africans will need to apply in advance for a Schengen visa which permits entry into Spain and other Schengen countries for 90 days in each six-month period.

For Morocco: British, EU, US, Canadian and Scandinavian passport holders can stay up to 90 days without a visa. Australian, New Zealand and South African passport holders need a visa, which can be obtained at the point of arrival into Morocco. Other nationalities need to obtain a visa from the Moroccan Consulate in their country of residence before departure. Israeli nationals are not permitted to enter Morocco at all.

Driving licence: If you are planning to hire a car while you are away, you will also need your UK or international driving licence, which must be carried in the car with you at all times.

MONEY
Currency
Gibraltar uses pounds sterling (£), available in £50, £20, £10 and £5 notes, and £2 and £1 coins. £1 is divided into 100 pence (p), available as 1, 2, 5, 10, 20 and 50 pence coins. Currency from mainland UK is legal tender in Gibraltar, but Gibraltar's currency – which features pictures of monkeys, the Rock and a visibly younger-looking Queen – cannot be used elsewhere, and will attract a lower rate of exchange in Spain and Morocco. Any bank or shop will be happy to swap local currency for mainland UK currency before you leave.

In Spain, the currency is the euro (€), available in 500, 200, 100, 50, 20, 10 and 5 euro notes and 1 and 2 euro coins. It is divided into 100 céntimos, which are available as 1, 2, 5, 10, 20 and 50 céntimo coins. Many shops do not accept 500 and 200 euro notes because of the risk of counterfeit currency.

The local currency in Morocco is the dirham (MAD). It is divided into 100 centimes, also referred to as francs. The importation or exportation of dirham is prohibited so technically you need to change money on arrival and to change all your dirham when you leave – although in practice some bureaux de change in Gibraltar, Algeciras and Tarifa will do the honours. Notes come in MAD 200, 100, 50, 20 and 10 denominations, and coins come as MAD 10, 5 and 1. Keep an eye out for counterfeit currency, which is occasionally passed on by unofficial moneychangers.

Banks In Gibraltar, banks are open for business 09.00–15.30 Monday–Thursday and 09.00–17.00 Friday. They are closed at the weekend. In Andalucía, banks are open 08.30–14.00 Monday–Friday and 08.30–13.00 Saturday during the winter. From May to September, they do not open on Saturdays.

Exchange bureaux Look out for the sign 'Cambio'; these are generally open seven days a week 10.00–21.00 but hours vary widely. There is one usefully placed at Gibraltar Airport, for use by those crossing the frontier.

Credit cards All major credit cards are widely accepted, but cash is preferred for smaller purchases and in more rural areas of Spain. Holders of Visa and MasterCard can use the plentiful 24-hour automatic cash dispensers (ATMs), which have instructions in English.

ATMs There are ATMs at all Spanish airports, but it can be a good idea to get hold of some euros from your local bank or the bureau de change at your departure airport to save you the hassle of hunting one down when you arrive.

Safety

The safest way to carry large amounts of money is as traveller's cheques (which are refunded in the event that they are lost or stolen) or to withdraw cash directly from your account using ATMs as you go. Most UK banks charge a minimum fee for overseas withdrawals – even in Gibraltar – so it is cheaper to withdraw fewer large amounts than lots of small ones. Before you go, contact your card providers and let them know you will be travelling abroad; otherwise they may assume your card details have been stolen and suspend your account. If you use your debit or credit cards to pay for things directly in Spain, be aware that you may be asked to validate purchases with a signature and your pin code. Most shops also request a passport as proof of identity.

CLIMATE

Gibraltar and the surrounding area is reliably sunny all year round, but it's at its best for beach holidays from the beginning of June to the end of August, when average temperatures range from 28°C (82°F) to 40°C (104°F) and there is very little rainfall. However, inland destinations can be unbearably hot at this time of year as the mercury zooms well over 40°C (104°F) without the sea breeze to cool things down. The region is much less busy in spring and autumn, and these can be lovely seasons to visit, with temperatures regularly climbing into the 20s°C (70s°F) but still cool enough to sightsee and sit out in the sun without burning. The winter sees a bit more rain and will often demand a coat, but the weather is still relatively mild with average temperatures from 8°C (46°F) to 17°C (63°F).

The other factor to take into account is the direction of the wind: in Gibraltar, an easterly wind (*levante*) usually forces moist sea air up over the Rock so that it forms a cloud that gets 'stuck' on the top (although along the Costa de la Luz, the *levante* is associated with sunny weather), while a westerly wind (*poniente*) often makes it overcast. Ask locals for advice if you are unsure.

Along this stretch of coast you should also pay attention to the force of the wind by checking out the latest conditions on websites like Ⓦ http://tarifa.costasur.com/en/weather.html. A good day in Tarifa is well worth the effort, but a blowy day on the beach will leave you feeling rather windswept.

BAGGAGE ALLOWANCE

Baggage allowances vary according to the airline, the destination and the class of travel, but most airlines allow each passenger to take one piece of luggage weighing up to 20 kg (44 lb) to be carried in the hold. You are also allowed one item of cabin baggage weighing no more than 5 kg (11 lb), and measuring 55 by 40 by 20 cm (22 × 16 × 8 in). Under current security rules, a woman's handbag counts as the item of cabin baggage and all liquids must be under 100 ml and carried separately in a see-through sealable bag. Large items – surfboards, golf clubs and collapsible wheelchairs – are often charged as extras, and it is a good idea to let the airline know in advance that you want to bring these.

During your stay

AIRPORTS

Gibraltar Airport This tiny airport is well placed for visiting the western edge of the Costa del Sol, and will be even better suited by mid-2011 when a new terminal is constructed with a direct exit to Spain. The expansion plans will also see a boost to the number of flights and services, although most major car-rental companies are already represented. There are nearly always taxis in front of the building to take you into Gibraltar, or you can take a red bus from just opposite the airport into Gibraltar's town centre. There are more taxis just the other side of the border for journeys further afield to the Costa del Sol. A 'Portillo' bus runs from the terminal in La Línea to Málaga, making a number of coastal stops. Estepona is about 30 minutes' drive away and Málaga is just over an hour away.

Málaga Airport Located 8 km (5 miles) southwest of Málaga city, this is the Costa del Sol's busiest airport by far. All major car-hire companies are represented and taxis are available from just outside the arrivals hall. Public transport connections are also good: buses run every half-hour 06.30–23.30 daily to the main bus terminal in Málaga city, where there are connections to Estepona, Fuengirola, La Línea (for Gibraltar), Mijas and Ronda, and throughout the region. Direct buses run between the airport and Marbella every 45 minutes between 06.15 and 23.45 daily. There is also an excellent train service between Málaga city and Fuengirola, (via the airport, Torremolinos and Arroyo de la Miel) which operates every 30 minutes (06.45–23.00 daily) and takes 42 minutes in total.

Sevilla Airport Located about 10 km (6 miles) northwest of Sevilla and about three hours' drive from Málaga, this airport is well served by car-hire companies and rail links to Málaga as well as to Madrid and Algeciras (just east of Gibraltar).

Jerez Airport Full car-hire facilities and taxis to local destinations are available from Jerez Airport. Daily buses run to Ronda, La Línea (for Gibraltar), Marbella and Málaga – a five-hour journey.

Useful advice on facilities available at all airports in Andalucia can be found at Ⓦ www.spanish-airport-guide.com

Tangier Airport About 6 km (3½ miles) from Tangier town.

COMMUNICATIONS
Telephones
Public telephones in Gibraltar are easy to use and easy to spot – in the traditional red telephone boxes that have long been associated with mainland UK. All accept coins and some accept cards. The prefix '200' was added in front of all telephone numbers in 2009 but not all listings have been updated.

In Spain, public telephones are mounted on posts or in glazed, silver *cabinas telefónicas* (phone booths). They accept coins and/or phonecards which can be purchased at newsstands and *estancos* (tobacconists), and many of them also have a button which you can press for instructions in English. Most have a list of international dialling codes, and useful numbers like the operator (1004) and directory services (1003). Alternatively, most restaurants and bars have a telephone available for public use.

Postal services
Gibraltar has bright red UK-style pillar boxes dotted around the city centre and there is a post office on Main Street where you can buy stamps. However, the postal service can be pretty sluggish. All incoming parcels must be collected in person from the depot and opened in front of an official. In Spain, postboxes are bright yellow and can be found at railway stations and post offices (*correos*) as well as dotted around town. Stamps (*sellos*) can be bought from post offices or tobacconists (*estancos*), which display a distinctive red-and-yellow sign and often have weighing

facilities too. The postal service itself is renowned for being slow and unreliable, with postcards to Europe taking up to a month to arrive because postboxes are sometimes not emptied for days. For the most reliable service, post letters at the post office itself or use the *certificado* (registered) and *urgente* (express) mail. Main post offices are open 08.30–20.30 Monday–Friday, 09.30–14.00 Saturday, closed Sunday.

Internet access
Internet cafés are readily available in the big tourist centres but can be hard to find in smaller towns or off the beaten track.

CUSTOMS
Introductions
When you are introduced to friends in Gibraltar or Spain, it is customary for women to offer a kiss on both cheeks, and for men to offer a kiss to women or to shake hands with men. Local men who know each other well often greet each other with a hug. However, most Spanish and Gibraltarian people know that this is not customary for all nationalities and will often offer a hand if they know you come from abroad.

Complaints
If you are not happy with a service in Spain, particularly in a restaurant or hotel, you are entitled to ask for the *Libro de Reclamaciones*. This is an official complaints book at the disposal of customers, which is inspected periodically by the local authorities. Only use it for very unsatisfactory affairs or just threaten to use it if you suspect you are being cheated.

DRESS CODES
Dress codes in Gibraltar and Spain are pretty relaxed. Spanish men tend to wear short-sleeved collared shirts or polo shirts, but T-shirts are just as acceptable. Women, meanwhile, have a love affair with lycra, and small, strappy tops are de rigueur for the young – usually teamed with heels and big earrings. Slightly older women go in for tailoring and are a little more covered up, with grooming high on the agenda. Both men and

women dress up a bit more in the evening and also to attend church. Topless sunbathing is not acceptable in Gibraltar, but it is okay in Spain on beaches away from town centres. Locals don't take too kindly to tourists wearing beach clothes in town, so be sensitive to this and cover up even if others don't.

In Morocco, dress codes are much more conservative. Men are advised to wear T-shirts and long shorts, while women should cover their legs to at least below the knee, as well as their shoulders and cleavage. Low-cut or strappy tops will attract a lot of hassle.

ELECTRICITY

Gibraltar runs on a 240 V current, and uses the same rectangular three-pin plug that is standard in mainland UK. The current in Spain and Morocco is 220 V-AC, and two-pin, round-pronged plugs are standard. Adaptors can be found in many hypermarkets, supermarkets and also some electrical stores. If you can, take one with you to be on the safe side. Most hotels and *pensiones* have electric points for hair dryers and shavers in all the bedrooms. If you are considering buying electrical appliances to take home, always check that they will work in your country before you buy.

EMERGENCIES

For urgent police, fire or ambulance assistance in Gibraltar or Spain, call 112. In Morocco, the emergency number for the police is 19 and for fire or ambulance assistance is 15.

Medical emergencies In case of a medical emergency, head to the nearest *Urgencias* – the emergency ward of a hospital or clinic. Gibraltar has a new state-of-the-art hospital at Europort. The Costa del Sol has a hospital with English-speaking staff situated on the main coastal highway (N340) just east of Marbella (Hospital Costa del Sol, Carretera Nacional N340, Km 187, Marbella,

Málaga). All cities in Spain have at least one hospital, and most have volunteer interpreters who speak English and occasionally also other languages.

If you need to use your EHIC card, do not part with the original but hand over a photocopy instead. If you have private travel insurance, make sure you have your policy on you when requesting medical assistance. Depending on the insurance company, you may be expected to pay for treatment and be reimbursed at a later date.

For minor emergencies, staff at pharmacies or *farmacias* will be able to suggest remedies for medical problems. They are open 09.30–13.30, 17.00–20.30 Monday–Friday and are easily recognised by a large green or red cross. After these times and on Saturdays and Sundays, there will always be a 'duty' chemist open, details of which will be posted on every chemist's window or, in Gibraltar, in the *Gibraltar Chronicle*.

Police

The Gibraltar police operate in exactly the same way (and wear exactly the same uniform) as in mainland UK, with one force responsible for all types of crime. In Spain, there are three types of police: the Guardia Civil, the Policía Nacional and the Policía Local. The Policía Nacional, who wear a blue uniform, are the best to turn to when reporting a crime. When approaching them, remember that it is illegal to be without ID.

Consulates

The British Consulate is at @ Plaza Nueva 87, 41001 Sevilla ❶ 954 22 88 74 and @ Calle Mauricio Moro Pareto 2, Málaga ❶ 952 35 23 00. The British Consulate in Tangier is at @ 9 Rue d'Amerique du Sud ❶ 039 93 69 39.

GETTING AROUND
Car hire & driving

All the major international car-hire companies operate in Gibraltar and Spain, and a few Spanish companies, such as Atesa, are also represented. You can probably negotiate the best deal with an international company from home before you go. There are also fly-drive and other package deals, including car hire. Fly-drive, an option for two or more travellers, can be arranged by travel agents. There are car-hire desks at airports and offices in the large towns. Alternatively, if you wish to hire a car locally for, say, a week or less, you can arrange it with a local travel agent. A car for hire is called a *coche de alquiler* in Spanish. Car-hire prices and conditions vary according to the region and locality.

Visitors driving vehicles from other countries need no special documentation in Spain, but make sure you have all the relevant papers from your country of origin: your driving licence, vehicle registration document and insurance. Your insurance company should be able to arrange an overseas extension of your car insurance.

To hire a car in Spain, you need show only a current driving licence. When driving from Britain, if you have an old-style green licence you will need to purchase an International Driving Permit, obtained from the RAC or the AA.

Most Spanish motorways are well equipped with an SOS network of telephones, which provide instant access to the emergency services. Ask for *auxilio en carretera*. In Spain, Gibraltar and Morocco, people drive on the right so you must give way to the right. At roundabouts, you should give way to cars already on the roundabout but be extremely careful when on a roundabout yourself: do not expect oncoming cars to stop. Some will disregard you and drive straight on.

The speed limits are 50 km/h (30 mph) in built-up areas; 90–100 km/h (55–60 mph) outside them and 120 km/h (75 mph) on motorways.

Seat belts are compulsory in the back and front; motor-cyclists must wear crash helmets. Drivers must carry two warning triangles and can be fined by the traffic police for not being equipped with a first-aid kit.

Taxis

Taxis in Gibraltar are abundant when you don't need one and thin on the ground when you do. They can be called but it is generally easier to pick one up at the nearest rank, for example in Grand Casemates Square. They are also the easiest way of visiting the Upper Rock, although tourists pay a different rate to locals for the tour and it can prove expensive. Beware of taxi drivers who claim the (cheaper) cable car is not working. Taxis are essential in Spain for access to out-of-town nightspots. You can phone from your hotel reception area, walk to a taxi rank, or flag one down as it passes by. A green light in the front window or on top of the roof indicates that the taxi is available for hire. Taxis are always white and have a logo on the doors, which displays their official number. Drivers in Spain rarely speak any English, so learn enough Spanish to explain where you are going and to negotiate the fare. The meter marks up the basic fare; however, supplements may be added for *tarifa nocturna* (night driving), *maletas* (luggage) or *días festivos* (public holidays). If in doubt of the correct price, ask for the *tarifas* (price list).

Public transport

Buses Regular double-decker buses run from Gibraltar town centre to the frontier with Spain, while slightly less frequent blue, single deckers ply other routes linking all the main beaches and residential areas.

In Spain, various private bus companies provide regular links between major resorts and outlying villages, including Portillo, one of the largest, which covers the Costa del Sol (Ⓦ www.ctsa-portillo.com). Buses run frequently (every 20–30 minutes) within and between resorts and are reasonably priced. Board buses at the front, and get off at the rear of the bus. You usually buy your ticket from the driver, or you can buy strips of ten tickets called *bonobus* from *estancos* (tobacconists) and stationers. It is not unusual for buses to be crowded.

Trains An excellent train service, with air conditioning and announcements in Spanish and English, runs between Málaga and Fuengirola, stopping at the airport, Torremolinos and Arroyo de la Miel.

⬤ An aerial view from the east side of the Rock

Trains operate every 30 minutes at the airport, in either direction, daily from 06.45 to 23.00. The full journey takes 42 minutes.

HEALTH, SAFETY & CRIME

It is fine to drink Gibraltan tap water but in Spain it is a good idea to stick to bottled water at all times, especially in the summer when the river beds dry up and cause pollutants in the water system to become concentrated. Food in Gibraltar and Spain is as reliable as anywhere else in Europe. Be sensible when eating in Morocco and eat at restaurants that have a high turnover of customers and look clean.

Crime is not a major problem, but travellers visiting busy markets should take basic precautions against pickpockets. Use prepaid cards or credit cards rather than cash, and carry a photocopy of your passport, leaving the original in the hotel safe. If you have a car, do not leave valuables in view, and try to leave it in a security-controlled car park. Report any incident to the police (*poner una denuncia*) as soon as possible (at least within 24 hours). This is extremely important if you wish to obtain a statement (*denuncia*) to make an insurance claim.

The abundance of street-life means that you will rarely find yourself alone or in a position to be harassed. However, women may be intimidated by men passing comment as they walk by, or even following them. This pastime, known as *piropo*, is common and not meant as a serious threat. Do not stop to use maps late at night, and try to look like you know where you are going. Make sure that you take official taxis displaying a licence number, and avoid public transport at night if alone. Any cab driver touting for business is likely to be illegal.

When in the countryside, you may see signs showing a bull or saying *Toro bravo* (fighting bull). Take these signs seriously – bulls are extremely dangerous and should certainly not be approached.

The biggest danger you are likely to face is overexposure to the sun, particularly from May to October, when temperatures can reach up to 45°C (113°F). Avoid walking in the midday sun, drink plenty of bottled mineral water and stay in the shade whenever possible.

Gibraltar's Catholic cathedral

OPENING HOURS

Shops Spanish shops tend to close during the afternoon siesta and on Sundays (except for department stores and touristy souvenir shops in the large towns). Most shops open at 09.30 and close at 13.30. They usually reopen about 17.00 or 17.30 and stay open until 20.30 or 21.00. These times will vary from shop to shop. In Gibraltar, hours are as in the UK, from 09.00 to 17.30, though many close on Sundays if there are no cruise ships in port.

Museums Hours kept by monuments and museums vary considerably, so it is best to check before you visit. Most close on Sunday afternoons. However, during the tourist season many of the more popular museums stay open all day.

Churches Most churches open only for Mass, but in small towns a caretaker will often let visitors in between religious services. In most churches, tourists are welcome in the church during a service as long as they are quiet. Dress codes are not as strict as in other Catholic countries, but avoid skimpy shorts and bare arms. There is usually no admission charge, although a donation may be expected.

Banks In Gibraltar, banks are open for business 09.00–15.30 Monday–Thursday and 09.00–17.00 Friday. They are closed at the weekend. In Andalucía, banks are open 08.30–14.00 Monday–Friday, and 08.30–13.00 Saturday during the winter. From May to September, they do not open on Saturdays. Banks are never open on public holidays, and during a town's annual *feria* week the banks will open for just three hours (09.00–12.00), to allow staff to join in the merrymaking.

RELIGION

Gibraltar is largely Catholic with significant Jewish and Muslim populations. Spain is predominantly Catholic and Morocco is Muslim.

SMOKING

In 2011, Spain introduced strict new laws banning smoking in all restaurants, bars and airports. However, at the time of writing, Gibraltar's smoking laws are much more lax.

TIME DIFFERENCES

Gibraltar and Spain are one hour ahead of Greenwich Mean Time (GMT) and British Summer Time. Morocco is on GMT.

In Spain, the 24-hour clock is used in listings and for official purposes, but not in speech.

TIPPING

Tipping tends to be an issue of discretion in Gibraltar and Spain. A service charge (*servicio*) is usually included in bills, but it is common to tip up to 10 per cent in addition and to give small change to petrol-pump attendants, taxi drivers, porters and parking attendants.

TOILETS

Public toilets are scarce, but bars and restaurants in Gibraltar are usually happy to allow you to use theirs, and those in Spain are legally bound to do so. A 'D' on the door stands for *Damas* (ladies), and a 'C' indicates *Caballeros* (men). Keep small change handy because if the toilets are not coin-operated, it is usual to leave some coins for the attendant. In Morocco, toilets are often the squat variety and vary in standards of cleanliness, so use your judgement. Although most smart hotels have Western-style facilities, always carry some toilet paper with you, as it is rarely supplied.

TRAVELLERS WITH DISABILITIES

Modern buildings generally have adequate provision for people with disabilities, with lifts, ramps and special toilet facilities. However, owing to their construction, entry to certain historical monuments may be restricted. Local tourist offices, or the monument staff, can provide up-to-date information about wheelchair access.

ACKNOWLEDGEMENTS

The publishers would like to thank the following individuals and organisations for supplying their copyright photographs for this book. BigStockPhoto (freeflyer) page 25; Dreamstime (Cleaper) pages 9 & 97, (Nick Stubbs) pages 38, 48, 120, (Scottwylie) page 122; Pictures Colour Library pages 5, 10–11, 20, 30, 33, 40, 44, 59, 60, 87, 101; Katherine Rushton pages 69, 71, 85; Lewis Stagnetto pages 13 & 89; Photoshot/World Pictures pages 22, 35, 68, 74, 79, 90; Thomas Cook Tour Operations Ltd pages 55, 62, 102; TIPS Images/Photononstop page 103; Wikimedia Commons (Nathan Harig) page 94.

Project editor: Thomas Willsher
Layout: Donna Pedley
Proofreaders: Cath Senker & Kelly Walker
Indexer: Marie Lorimer

Send your thoughts to
books@thomascook.com

- Found a beach bar, peaceful stretch of sand or must-see sight that we don't feature?

- Like to tip us off about any information that needs a little updating?

- Want to tell us what you love about this handy little guidebook and, more importantly, how we can make it even handier?

Then here's your chance to tell all! Send us ideas, discoveries and recommendations today and then look out for your valuable input in the next edition of this title.

Email to the above address or write to:
pocket guides Series Editor, Thomas Cook Publishing, PO Box 227, Unit 9, Coningsby Road, Peterborough PE3 8SB, UK.

Useful phrases

English	Spanish	Approx pronunciation
BASICS		
Yes	Sí	*Si*
No	No	*Noh*
Please	Por favor	*Por fabor*
Thank you	Gracias	*Grathias*
Hello	Hola	*Ola*
Goodbye	Adiós	*Adios*
Excuse me	Disculpe	*Diskoolpeh*
Sorry	Perdón	*Pairdohn*
That's okay	De acuerdo	*Dey acwerdo*
I don't speak Spanish	No hablo español	*Noh ablo espanyol*
Do you speak English?	¿Habla Usted inglés?	*¿Abla oosteth eengless?*
Good morning	Buenos días	*Bwenos dee-as*
Good afternoon	Buenas tardes	*Bwenas tarrdess*
Good evening	Buenas noches	*Bwenas notchess*
Goodnight	Buenas noches	*Bwenas notchess*
My name is ...	Me llamo ...	*Meh yiamo ...*
NUMBERS		
One	Uno	*Oono*
Two	Dos	*Dos*
Three	Tres	*Tres*
Four	Cuatro	*Cwatro*
Five	Cinco	*Thinco*
Six	Seis	*Seys*
Seven	Siete	*Seeyetey*
Eight	Ocho	*Ocho*
Nine	Nueve	*Nwebeyh*
Ten	Diez	*Deeyeth*
Twenty	Veinte	*Beintey*
Fifty	Cincuenta	*Thincwenta*
One hundred	Cien	*Thien*
SIGNS & NOTICES		
Airport	Aeropuerto	*Aehropwerto*
Railway station	Estación de trenes	*Estathion de trenes*
Platform	Vía	*Vía*
Smoking/	Fumadores/	*Foomadoores/*
non-smoking	No fumadores	*No foomadores*
Toilets	Servicios	*Serbitheeos*
Ladies/Gentlemen	Señoras/Caballeros	*Senyoras/Kabayeros*